OSAT®

Middle Level English Practice Questions

I0877308

OSAT, CEOE, Oklahoma Subject Area Tests, and Certification Examinations for Oklahoma Educators are trademarks of the Office of Educational Quality and Accountability and Pearson Education, Inc. or its affiliate(s). This product was developed by Mometrix Test Preparation. It was not developed in connection with Pearson Education, Inc., nor was it reviewed, approved or endorsed by these agencies.

Mometrix
TEST PREPARATION

Dear Future Exam Success Story

First of all, **THANK YOU** for purchasing Mometrix study materials!

Second, congratulations! You are one of the few determined test-takers who are committed to doing whatever it takes to excel on your exam. **You have come to the right place.** We developed these practice tests with one goal in mind: to deliver you the best possible approximation of the questions you will see on test day.

Standardized testing is one of the biggest obstacles on your road to success, which only increases the importance of doing well in the high-pressure, high-stakes environment of test day. Your results on this test could have a significant impact on your future, and these practice tests will give you the repetitions you need to build your familiarity and confidence with the test content and format to help you achieve your full potential on test day.

Your success is our success

We would love to hear from you! If you would like to share the story of your exam success or if you have any questions or comments in regard to our products, please contact us at **800-673-8175** or **support@mometrix.com**.

Thanks again for your business and we wish you continued success!

Sincerely,
The Mometrix Test Preparation Team

Copyright © 2026 by Mometrix Media LLC. All rights reserved.
Printed in the United States of America

Table of Contents

Practice Test #1

Multiple Choice

1. Which of the following is an accurate statement about text coding (Harvey and Daniels, 2009) as an active reading strategy?

a. Text coding refers to having students write computer code.
b. Text coding is a strategy that some also call text monitoring.
c. Text coding and text monitoring are two different strategies.
d. Text coding can be done by students with no teacher model.

2. Archie says, "Northerners eat bland food." Which of the following terms most precisely describes the thought Archie expresses?

a. Stereotype
b. Inference
c. Assumption
d. Generalization

3. W. H. Auden's poem "As I Walked Out One Evening" (1940) includes this stanza:

I'll love you till the ocean
Is folded and hung up to dry
And the seven stars go squawking
Like geese about the sky.

Which of the following literary devices is NOT used in this stanza?

a. Simile
b. Paradox
c. Hyperbole
d. Alliteration

4. Which of the following is NOT a criterion for evaluating the strength of an analysis that is based on textual evidence?

a. The analysis explains the author's intended meaning or purpose.
b. The analysis uses strong, relevant, and accurate evidence for support.
c. The analysis includes specific evidence, such as paraphrasing or direct quotes.
d. The analysis shows special insight into a theme, character, or story event.

5. Which of the following statements is correct regarding how teachers must respond to students' individual and group identities and needs in inclusive educational programs?

a. Teachers must meet student needs rather than student family needs.
b. Teachers must meet student needs but not express their own needs.
c. Teachers must meet their own needs through team problem-solving.
d. Teachers must meet their own needs through independent solutions.

Copyright © Mometrix Media. You have been licensed one copy of this document for personal use only. Any other reproduction or redistribution is strictly prohibited. All rights reserved.
This content is provided for test preparation purposes only and does not imply an endorsement by Mometrix of any particular political, scientific, or religious point of view.

6. In comparing and contrasting the sonnet and the ballad as subgenres of the literary genre of poetry, which of these do both forms have in common?

a. They both have five main kinds.
b. They both often express love.
c. They both began with music.
d. They both have equal meter.

7. In Kate Chopin's short story "The Story of an Hour" (1894), Chopin's description of Louise Mallard as "young, with a fair, calm face, whose lines bespoke repression and even a certain strength" contributes to her character development to help explain which plot event most?

a. Her reaction to seeing her husband alive.
b. The controlling behavior of her husband.
c. Why her immediate grief ended so soon.
d. Her joy when her husband was not dead.

8. What do the books *Pamela* and *Clarissa* by Samuel Richardson; *Dangerous Liaisons* by Pierre Choderlos de Laclos; *The Sorrows of Young Werther* by Johann Wolfgang von Goethe; *The History of Emily Montague* by Frances Brooke; and *Frankenstein* by Mary Shelley all have in common?

a. They are all picaresque novels.
b. They are all first novels in their countries.
c. They are all novels written in epistolary form.
d. They are all novels written in the 18th century.

9. If a student has an assignment to speak before the whole class on a given topic and include a visual aid, which of the following technological tools would be most appropriate?

a. A slide show
b. A poster
c. A blog
d. A wiki

10. Which of the following sentences uses correct grammar and punctuation?

a. Those gloves are her's, but the Browns say that book is their's.
b. Those gloves are hers, but the Brown's say that book is theirs.
c. Those gloves are her's, but the Brown's say that book is their's.
d. Those gloves are hers, but the Browns say that book is theirs.

11. In a rough draft of an essay, a student has written, "My best friend Gina is a wonderful athlete, a wonderful student, a wonderful person, and a wonderful friend." Which online reference should she consult to improve this description?

a. A grammar guide
b. An encyclopedia
c. A dictionary
d. A thesaurus

Copyright © Mometrix Media. You have been licensed one copy of this document for personal use only. Any other reproduction or redistribution is strictly prohibited. All rights reserved.
This content is provided for test preparation purposes only and does not imply an endorsement by Mometrix of any particular political, scientific, or religious point of view.

12. Use the following sentence to answer this question.

After we arrive, we will split up into small groups to tour the museum separately.

In this sentence, which part is a prepositional phrase?

a. after we arrive
b. split up
c. into small groups
d. to tour

13. Which of the following is NOT a clause?

a. He died.
b. It's raining.
c. A very good time
d. Then we went out

14. In the steps that a reader can follow to evaluate an informational text writer's arguments, which should come first?

a. Identifying the conclusion the argument makes
b. Judging the validity or supportiveness of premises
c. Clarifying premises or reasons with paraphrases
d. Identifying the supporting premises or reasons

15. Regarding organization, what statement is most accurate about outlines relative to writing?

a. Outlining is only for student writers.
b. Outlines are for professional writers.
c. Outlines are for planning, not analyzing.
d. Outlines aid in planning and analysis.

16. When writing an essay, which of the following attributes belongs in the introduction?

a. Getting the reader's attention
b. Developing the thesis statement
c. Giving examples of the thesis idea
d. Giving the reader a sense of closure

17. Which of the following is most accurate regarding the sequence of steps a reader should take to evaluate arguments in an informational text?

a. Readers should find supporting premises and only look for the conclusion once these are understood.
b. Readers should first identify an argument's conclusion and then identify the premises supporting it.
c. Readers should note an argument's conclusion and supporting premises in the order they are presented.
d. Readers should try to paraphrase premises to clarify them, not to make them fit with the conclusion.

Copyright © Mometrix Media. You have been licensed one copy of this document for personal use only. Any other reproduction or redistribution is strictly prohibited. All rights reserved.
This content is provided for test preparation purposes only and does not imply an endorsement by Mometrix of any particular political, scientific, or religious point of view.

18. In which of the following literary forms is the element of literary devices such as similes, metaphors, personification, etc. *most* prominent?

a. Plays
b. Poems
c. Nonfiction
d. Short stories

19. Regarding research-based instructional strategies for collaborative student writing groups, what is correct about developing and setting goals?

a. Setting specific goals for writing undermines student motivation.
b. Only the teachers should develop writing goals for the students.
c. Teachers should expect students to develop their writing goals.
d. Both the teachers and the students may develop writing goals.

Refer to the following for questions 20–23:

The Thought-Fox

I imagine this midnight moment's forest:
Something else is alive
Beside the clock's loneliness
And this blank page where my fingers move.
Through the window I see no star:
Something more near
Though deeper within darkness
Is entering the loneliness:
Cold, delicately as the dark snow
A fox's nose touches twig, leaf;
Two eyes serve a movement, that now
And again now, and now, and now
Sets neat prints into the snow
Between trees, and warily a lame
Shadow lags by stump and in hollow
Of a body that is bold to come
Across clearings, an eye,
A widening deepening greenness,
Brilliantly, concentratedly,
Coming about its own business
Till, with a sudden sharp hot stink of fox,
It enters the dark hole of the head.
The window is starless still; the clock ticks,
The page is printed.

From *Ted Hughes: Selected Poems 1957-1967. Copyright © 1972 by Ted Hughes, Harper & Row Publishers, Inc.*

20. Which of the following best summarizes the creative writing process as described by the poem?

a. The writer carefully guides a thought.
b. The writer looks to nature for a thought.
c. The poet imagines a fox to help him to write.
d. The writer is a passive recipient of a thought.

Copyright © Mometrix Media. You have been licensed one copy of this document for personal use only. Any other reproduction or redistribution is strictly prohibited. All rights reserved.
This content is provided for test preparation purposes only and does not imply an endorsement by Mometrix of any particular political, scientific, or religious point of view.

21. Which of the following literary devices is primarily used by the poet in this work?

a. Foreshadowing
b. Repetition
c. Metaphor
d. Irony

22. In which of the following forms is this poem written?

a. Free verse
b. Blank verse
c. Rhymed verse
d. Metered verse

23. Which of these does the poem describe?

a. The process of observing a fox
b. The process of being inspired to write
c. The process of passing the time by thinking
d. The process of creating art from seeing nature

24. In the Gilgamesh Epic, the Islamic Quran, and the Old Testament book of Genesis, which of the following most represents a universal theme they commonly share?

a. A flood occurring all over the world and destroying everybody.
b. A flood as God's way to eliminate humans behaving wickedly.
c. A flood before which a man is told to build a ship to escape it.
d. A flood after which a survivor sends birds out to test its end.

25. Two groups of students are assigned to compare texts. One group is given speeches by Abraham Lincoln and Stephen Douglas about slavery. The other group is given essays by an author from the Enlightenment and one from the Romantic movement about nature. What are the students most likely to conclude?

a. Both groups will find that both texts conflict.
b. One pair of texts will conflict; one will agree.
c. Both groups will find both texts to be similar.
d. One pair of texts differs greatly; one differs slightly.

26. Identify the grammatical error in the following sentence:

They liked to stay at home, cook dinner, and watching TV.

a. Lack of parallelism
b. Split infinitive
c. Squinting modifier
d. Subject-verb disagreement

27. When asking a research question, which of the following should a researcher do first?

a. Search the literature for knowledge gaps related to the topic
b. Search the literature for definitive answers to that question
c. Search the literature for additional research needs or openings
d. Search the literature for consensus or controversy on the topic

Copyright © Mometrix Media. You have been licensed one copy of this document for personal use only. Any other reproduction or redistribution is strictly prohibited. All rights reserved.
This content is provided for test preparation purposes only and does not imply an endorsement by Mometrix of any particular political, scientific, or religious point of view.

28. Among these advantages of using digital media in education, which is most closely connected to reflecting individual differences among students?

a. Rapid navigation among multiple media
b. More diverse formats and experiences
c. Constant or frequent real-time updates
d. Global access to information and people

29. As an example of figurative language, who first used the "ship of state" metaphor?

a. Longfellow
b. Aeschylus
c. Alcaeus
d. Plato

30. Common standards for middle school grades include evaluating textual arguments and claims. Within this standard, which of the following is an element applying uniquely to the eighth grade?

a. Tracing/delineating and evaluating argument and specific claims in a text
b. Distinguishing claims supported by evidence and reasons versus being unsupported
c. Assessing whether reasoning is sound and evidence is relevant and sufficient
d. Recognizing whether some evidence that has been introduced is irrelevant

31. Which choice is the most correct statement about mood and tone in literature?

a. Mood and tone are synonyms referring to the emotional atmosphere of the work.
b. Mood is the emotion evoked in the reader by the work; tone is the author's emotion.
c. Mood is the emotion expressed by a work's author; tone is the emotion evoked in the reader by the work.
d. Mood is established by authors using different literary techniques than those used in creating tone.

32. Which of the following techniques that writers can use to promote coherence in paragraphs best reinforces the importance of certain ideas?

a. Transition
b. Repetition
c. Parallelism
d. Consistency

33. Which of the following statements does NOT reflect research findings regarding the teaching of cognitive strategies to improve student writing?

a. Cognitive strategies are effective for students of all ages.
b. Cognitive strategies can be helpful in planning written compositions.
c. Cognitive strategies help less than metacognitive strategies.
d. Cognitive strategies benefit students regardless of their ability.

34. Based on research evidence, what do experts recommend to effectively instruct students in writing strategies?

a. Teachers should demonstrate strategies and then assign independent student practice.
b. Teachers should explain strategies and let students practice them without any models.
c. Teachers should model strategies, then guide practice, then give independent practice.
d. Teachers should first give students guided practice in strategies and then model them.

Copyright © Mometrix Media. You have been licensed one copy of this document for personal use only. Any other reproduction or redistribution is strictly prohibited. All rights reserved.
This content is provided for test preparation purposes only and does not imply an endorsement by Mometrix of any particular political, scientific, or religious point of view.

35. Which of the following is critically effective for the purposes and audiences of blog writing?

a. Writing with correct punctuation
b. Writing with longer paragraphs
c. Writing with longer sentences
d. Writing with smaller font size

36. Read the sentence below and use it to answer this question.

Because he was late, he missed the field trip, and this caused him to fail the class.

How many dependent and independent clauses does this sentence contain?

a. One dependent clause and one independent clause
b. Two dependent clauses and one independent clause
c. One dependent clause and two independent clauses
d. Two dependent clauses and two independent clauses

37. In his poem "As I Walked Out One Evening" (1940), W. H. Auden writes:

I'll love you, dear, I'll love you
Till China and Africa meet,
And the river jumps over the mountain
And the salmon sing in the street.

This stanza uses an example of which type of literary device/figurative language?

a. Hubris
b. Hyperbole
c. Hyperbaton
d. Hypophora

38. Which of the following statements is true about TV and radio as types of media for communicating ideas?

a. TV is a high-status mass medium, but radio is not.
b. TV does not have as broad of a reach as radio does.
c. TV and radio can both serve to raise awareness.
d. TV targets more specific audiences than radio.

39. What is one limitation of informal reading assessments?

a. They must be administered in a standardized fashion, increasing student anxiety.
b. The results may be subjective.
c. They require more time to plan and implement than formal assessments.
d. They are often costly to administer and score.

40. Two mothers of young children write their observations about parenting. Writer A publishes her writing daily for a wide reading audience. Writer B also writes daily, but privately. Which two forms of writing best identify their activities?

a. Blog; journal
b. Journal; letters
c. Letters; essays
d. Essays; speeches

Copyright © Mometrix Media. You have been licensed one copy of this document for personal use only. Any other reproduction or redistribution is strictly prohibited. All rights reserved.
This content is provided for test preparation purposes only and does not imply an endorsement by Mometrix of any particular political, scientific, or religious point of view.

41. Of the following attributes of mobile and text media for presenting ideas in public communications, which is a disadvantage?

a. Popularity
b. Timeliness
c. Interactivity
d. Limited length

42. Among these forms of electronic media, which have the highest level of formality?

a. Online news articles
b. Online blogs
c. Emails
d. All are the same

43. What does a writer do in the organization stage?

a. Determines the purpose, thesis, and supporting details of the written work
b. Brainstorms ideas for items to include in the written work
c. Submits the writing to a classmate for editing
d. Writes the introduction and conclusion

44. In *The Old Man and the Sea,* Hemingway begins, "He was an old man who fished alone in a skiff in the Gulf Stream and he had gone eighty-four days now without taking a fish." The primary meaning of this opening sentence is

a. symbolic
b. implied
c. literal
d. true

45. Suppose an informational text on the writer's craft presents a list of common errors in essay writing along with the consequences of these errors and steps writers can take in order to avoid committing these errors themselves. Which of these text structures would this informational text most likely follow?

a. Process narrative
b. Cause and effect
c. Problem-solution
d. Description

46. For which of the following purposes would a teacher use a formative assessment?

a. To get data to inform a school improvement plan
b. To get or keep government funding for the school
c. To get data about individual student performance
d. To get data on student progress over a school year

Copyright © Mometrix Media. You have been licensed one copy of this document for personal use only. Any other reproduction or redistribution is strictly prohibited. All rights reserved.
This content is provided for test preparation purposes only and does not imply an endorsement by Mometrix of any particular political, scientific, or religious point of view.

47. A telecommunications salesman is writing informational text to persuade customers to agree to buy the products and services he is selling. One tactic includes advising the customer, "You are hemorrhaging money!" This is an example of which method of persuasion?

a. A generalization
b. Using a metaphor
c. Rhetorical question
d. Negative connotation

48. Which of these is most accurate about the function of dialogue in fictional literature?

a. Dialogue can serve to advance the plot but not develop characters.
b. Dialogue can serve to illuminate themes and meanings and redirect plots.
c. Dialogue can serve to break up exposition and slow the pace of the story.
d. Dialogue can serve to reproduce real speech instead of adding drama.

49. Someone argues, "But if you legalize this drug, all drugs will be legalized." In rhetoric, this is an example of which type of logical fallacy?

a. Straw man
b. Red herring
c. Slippery slope
d. *Post hoc ergo propter hoc*

50. Teachers must establish clear ground rules before initiating class or group discussions to ensure that students practice active listening and productive participation. Which of the following rules is more applicable to young children and students with behavior disorders than to all students equally?

a. No cross-talk
b. No interrupting
c. No monopolizing discussions
d. No hitting, kicking, biting, etc.

51. Which statement most accurately represents how evidence-based instructional approaches should be evaluated for effectiveness?

a. During the evaluation, assessors define the teaching practices that were used.
b. Ongoing monitoring is unnecessary because the evaluation identifies practices.
c. Appropriate, established measures are used to evaluate student results.
d. Student progress can be assessed without comparing teaching methods.

52. Which statement is most accurate regarding journals as a form of writing?

a. Journals are only for confiding and processing personal experiences in private.
b. Journals entries should all open with a greeting.
c. Journals can serve as free practice for writers to develop their skills.
d. Journals may best serve as a therapy for the reader but not for the author.

53. Which of the following sentences uses metaphor to create figurative meanings?

a. He became a tiger in the boxing ring, but he turned into a pussycat at dinner afterward.
b. He was like a tiger in the boxing ring, but later during dinner, he was just like a pussycat.
c. He fought so fiercely in the boxing ring, but afterward at dinner he was gentle and kind.
d. He was ferocious when he was boxing, but he was sweet and gentle in social situations.

Copyright © Mometrix Media. You have been licensed one copy of this document for personal use only. Any other reproduction or redistribution is strictly prohibited. All rights reserved.
This content is provided for test preparation purposes only and does not imply an endorsement by Mometrix of any particular political, scientific, or religious point of view.

54. What statement is correct regarding effective teacher techniques for classroom discussions?

a. Teachers making comments instead of asking questions encourages creativity in student responses.
b. When some students dominate discussion, teachers engage others with more challenging questions.
c. To meet learning goals, teachers can redirect off-subject discussion by restating topics and questions.
d. A checklist based on the class attendance roll is not the best way to assess all students' participation.

55. Which choice describes the most complete method of displaying student achievement or progress in language arts?

a. A written report or story that demonstrates a student's knowledge of grammar, spelling, comprehension, and writing skills.
b. Either a norm- or criterion-referenced test that breaks language skills into small subsets and provides achievement levels for each skill.
c. A portfolio containing a log of stories or books the student has read, rates of reading fluency, writing samples, creative projects, and spelling, grammar, and comprehension tests/quizzes.
d. A year-end project in which the student presents what he or she has learned from a student-chosen book; the student must read an excerpt of the story and display a visual aid highlighting important information from the story or literary techniques used by the author.

56. In differentiated instruction classrooms, which is the most common type of differentiation?

a. The way individual students access content
b. The way that learning goals are assessed
c. The concepts individual students are taught
d. The amount of detail in teaching concepts

57. In his *Poetics*, Aristotle defines epic, comic, and tragic poetry genres. Subsequent scholars have altered these somewhat. Which three main poetry genres have they defined?

a. Epic, lyric, and dramatic poetry
b. Epic, comic, and tragic poetry
c. Dramatic, comic, and tragic
d. Lyric, tragic, and comedic

58. Which of the following purposes of writing is NOT a common purpose of journal writing?

a. Documenting experiences with an illness
b. Chronicling recovery from an addiction
c. Describing travels or figurative journeys
d. Relating stories of fictional characters

59. Of the following, which sentence is correctly punctuated?

a. "I told you that it would be ready next week; it will be ready next week."
b. "I told you, that it would be ready next week it will be ready next week."
c. "I told you that it would be ready next week, it will be ready next week."
d. "I told you that it would be ready next week it will be ready next week."

Copyright © Mometrix Media. You have been licensed one copy of this document for personal use only. Any other reproduction or redistribution is strictly prohibited. All rights reserved.
This content is provided for test preparation purposes only and does not imply an endorsement by Mometrix of any particular political, scientific, or religious point of view.

60. The active reading strategy of text coding or text monitoring involves which of these?

a. Students separate codes into two columns.
b. Students write main points on sticky notes.
c. Students summarize a text in notation form.
d. Students make notes in the margins of a text.

61. Read the sentence below and use it to answer this question.

Bess, who can draw beautifully, loves art; but Grace, who thinks very logically, prefers science.

Which of the following sentence structures is this sentence an example of?

a. Compound-complex
b. Compound
c. Complex
d. Simple

62. In digital media, which of these advantages do cross-media transformations provide?

a. Students can underline all summary sentences in detailed texts.
b. Teachers can italicize all words in a text with Greek or Latin roots.
c. Students can boldface new or unfamiliar vocabulary words in a text.
d. Teachers and students can convert speech to text and text to speech.

63. Maria's topic sentence is: "My family throws elaborate holiday celebrations." Which of the following would be the best supporting detail to follow that sentence?

a. Holidays are just a waste of everyone's time and money, in my opinion.
b. First, we decide who will host the holiday dinner and when the celebration will take place.
c. My household includes five people, but my extended family includes over thirty people.
d. Afterwards, we all help clean up and then relax by continuing to chat with each other.

64. The syllable *-tion* is a(n) _____ and turns a _____ into a ______.

a. suffix; verb; noun
b. affix; noun; pronoun
c. prefix; noun; verb
d. infix; noun; adjective

65. Suppose someone writes an expository essay arguing against legalizing one specific drug, basing this argument on the premise that its legalization will lead to more and more drugs being legalized until no drugs are illegal anymore. Which of the following logical fallacies has this writer committed?

a. Slippery slope
b. Non sequitur
c. Red herring
d. Straw man

66. Which of these literary masterpieces is NOT an epic poem?

a. Dante's *Divine Comedy*
b. Milton's *Paradise Lost*
c. James Joyce's *Ulysses*
d. Spenser's *The Faerie Queene*

Copyright © Mometrix Media. You have been licensed one copy of this document for personal use only. Any other reproduction or redistribution is strictly prohibited. All rights reserved.
This content is provided for test preparation purposes only and does not imply an endorsement by Mometrix of any particular political, scientific, or religious point of view.

67. The sentence, "After completing the assignment correctly, the teacher gave Peter a high grade" is an example of which kind of error?

a. A lack of parallelism
b. A sentence fragment
c. A dangling participle
d. A run-on sentence

Refer to the following for question 68:

> "Although we liked Bill and Hillary, we did not go to their party because there were too many people there for us."

68. In the sentence above, what is "Although we liked Bill and Hillary"?

a. A prepositional phrase
b. An independent clause
c. A dependent clause
d. A complete sentence

69. "Courage, determination, and perseverance is required for success in this effort." What is grammatically incorrect in this sentence?

a. There is nothing wrong
b. Subject-verb agreement
c. Agreement of verb tense
d. Lack of parallel structure

70. Among effective reading strategies, which one involves recalling relevant past experience and existing knowledge to construct meaning from the new information in text that one reads?

a. Inferring
b. Activating
c. Questioning
d. Summarizing

71. Shakespeare wrote in Act II, Scene VII of *As You Like It*: "All the world's a stage, /And all the men and women merely players;/They have their exits and their entrances;/And one man in his time plays many parts ...." His meaning here is ____________________.

a. primarily denotative
b. primarily connotative
c. half one, half the other
d. neither type of meaning

Copyright © Mometrix Media. You have been licensed one copy of this document for personal use only. Any other reproduction or redistribution is strictly prohibited. All rights reserved.
This content is provided for test preparation purposes only and does not imply an endorsement by Mometrix of any particular political, scientific, or religious point of view.

72. In his short story "The Tell-Tale Heart" (1843), Edgar Allan Poe writes in the main character's narration:

> How, then, am I mad? Harken! and observe how healthily—how calmly I can tell you the whole story... Now this is the point. You fancy me mad. Madmen know nothing. But you should have seen me. You should have seen how wisely I proceeded — with what caution — with what foresight — with what dissimulation I went to work! I was never kinder to the old man than during the whole week before I killed him.

What does Poe want readers to infer from this text?

a. The character is sane.
b. The character is mad.
c. The character is evil.
d. The character is clever.

73. Which of the following common modes of writing is most characterized by the author's assumption of certain facts or truths?

a. Informative
b. Descriptive
c. Persuasive
d. Narrative

74. Consider a paired reading exercise that aims to help students understand an informational text. Which of the following will be a necessary part of the exercise?

a. Identifying genres that the work fits into
b. Identifying the main idea and supporting details
c. Identifying prior knowledge that both students have
d. Identifying any external texts that support the author's view

75. In *Great Expectations,* among relationships involving conflicts that Dickens used to develop the theme of revenge, which choice correctly describes how revenge figured in the relationship?

a. Miss Havisham takes her revenge against Estella.
b. Estella takes her revenge against Miss Havisham.
c. Magwitch takes revenge against protagonist Pip.
d. Pip takes his revenge against the character Orlick.

76. Which of the following attempts to persuade readers by making a claim based on anecdotal or insufficient evidence?

a. Hasty generalization
b. Rhetorical questions
c. Transfer and association
d. Ad hominem attack

77. Which author's works have explored the experience and roles of black women in American society?

a. Toni Morrison
b. Washington Irving
c. Richard Wright
d. Flannery O'Conner

Copyright © Mometrix Media. You have been licensed one copy of this document for personal use only. Any other reproduction or redistribution is strictly prohibited. All rights reserved.
This content is provided for test preparation purposes only and does not imply an endorsement by Mometrix of any particular political, scientific, or religious point of view.

78. Which of the following statements is accurate regarding criteria for evaluating the credibility of websites as sources?

a. Who publishes or sponsors a web page is more important than its domain name.
b. Whether information can be verified supersedes the timeliness of page updates.
c. Users must be vigilant against writer and publisher bias.
d. Links to, citations of, and recommendations for other sources take away credibility.

79. Which of the following can the writer determine without considering the audience?

a. Purpose
b. Structure
c. Word choice
d. Amount of research

80. How would an author best use rhetoric to provide readers with supporting evidence of a main point in an informational text?

a. By evocative descriptions
b. By making good analogies
c. By telling personal stories
d. By reporting case studies

81. Which of the following is an appropriate criterion to consider when evaluating a student's summary of a passage from literature?

a. The summary should be concise, even at the expense of completeness.
b. The summary should include the reactions and opinions the reader had.
c. The summary should cover points in proportion to the reader's interest.
d. The summary should tag attributions, cite sources, and limit quotations.

82. Regarding literal versus figurative language in informational texts, the words "politician" and "statesman" have which of the following?

a. Both the same denotation and connotation
b. Both different denotations and connotations
c. The same denotation but different connotations
d. The same connotation but different denotations

83. "He could not finish the test in time even though he tried his hardest." This sentence is of which type?

a. Compound-complex
b. Compound
c. Complex
d. Simple

84. In an informational text, which of these is most likely to make use of the others?

a. Irony
b. Satire
c. Overstatement
d. Understatement

Copyright © Mometrix Media. You have been licensed one copy of this document for personal use only. Any other reproduction or redistribution is strictly prohibited. All rights reserved.
This content is provided for test preparation purposes only and does not imply an endorsement by Mometrix of any particular political, scientific, or religious point of view.

85. Of the following attributes of technical language used in informational texts, which represent(s) the character of the mood rather than the character of the tone?

a. Concise
b. Impersonal
c. Professional
d. Self-deprecating versus grandiose

86. If a student has a writing assignment, which of the following is true regarding his or her audience?

a. The student need not identify the audience because it is the teacher.
b. The student should consider the readers' purpose for reading and response to the writing.
c. The student should know his or her writing purpose and not be concerned with a reader's purposes.
d. The student can develop an audience profile but assume the main audience is the teacher.

87. Middle school students at Ms. Kelso's school are expected to complete a large independent study project to be presented at the end of the second term. The project is the culmination of reading research, writing a paper, and the final element of publishing, or presentation. The students can choose how they present their work and are instructed to use visual aids. Which of the following would be a helpful guideline for Ms. Kelso to offer her students?

a. Whenever possible, use pictures, video, music, charts and graphs to supplement your presentation for the purpose of keeping your audience's interest.
b. Think about any parts of your paper that might be hard to explain. Choose a visual aid to help you show your audience the concept, and then use your words to explain it.
c. Select the most interesting photographs from your research, create color photocopies, and pass them throughout the class during your presentation.
d. Use your main ideas and supporting evidence to create a Power-point slideshow, making note-taking and organization simple and clear.

88. Which of the following characteristics can the fiction subgenres of historical fiction and science fiction be said to share in common?

a. Both are always about fictional characters.
b. Both are always about imaginary events.
c. Both are always speculative in some way.
d. Both are always closely aligned with facts.

89. The sentence below exhibits which of the following grammatical errors?

For modern readers, the stories contained within the Arthurian legends are often most familiar because of English poet Alfred, Lord Tennyson, his *Idylls of the King* focuses largely on the romantic triangle of Arthur, Guinevere, and Lancelot.

a. Comma splice
b. Incorrect verb tense
c. Incorrect use of parallelism
d. There is no error

Copyright © Mometrix Media. You have been licensed one copy of this document for personal use only. Any other reproduction or redistribution is strictly prohibited. All rights reserved.
This content is provided for test preparation purposes only and does not imply an endorsement by Mometrix of any particular political, scientific, or religious point of view.

90. Which of the following considerations does NOT help readers infer the author's point of view or purpose in informational text where it is not explicitly stated?

a. What the author wants to accomplish by writing the text
b. How effective the author's selection and use of supporting evidence is
c. What the author wants to persuade readers to accept, agree with, or believe
d. How the author's word choice affects the reader's perceptions of the subject matter

91. For evaluating the credibility of a source when doing research, which of these is true?

a. The author's reputation is more important than whether s/he cites sources.
b. The source should always be as recent as possible, regardless of the subject.
c. The author's point of view and/or purpose is not relevant to the credibility.
d. The kinds of sources various audiences value influences credibility for them.

92. Among these literary genres, in which pair has one *most* been used within the other?

a. Nonfiction prose within poetry
b. Fictional prose within drama
c. Poetry within fictional drama
d. Poetry within nonfiction prose

93. What is correct about how teachers can use rubrics as a research-based assessment method?

a. Teachers should use rubrics to conduct formative (not summative) student work assessments.
b. Teachers should use rubrics for lesson objectives, both to guide and to assess students' work.
c. Teachers should use rubrics to conduct summative (not formative) student work assessments.
d. Teachers should use rubrics in place of stating learning objectives and modeling performance.

94. In his epic poem *The Song of Hiawatha* (1855), how does Henry Wadsworth Longfellow most use poetic devices?

a. He uses couplets to answer questions asked before.
b. He uses couplets to clarify development of a theme.
c. He uses meter that evokes the rhythms of chanting.
d. He uses irony to help in development of the theme.

Refer to the following for questions 95–97:

Because I could not stop for Death —
He kindly stopped for me —
The Carriage held but just Ourselves —
And Immortality.

We slowly drove — He knew no haste
And I had put away
My labor and my leisure too,
For His Civility —

We passed the School, where Children strove

Copyright © Mometrix Media. You have been licensed one copy of this document for personal use only. Any other reproduction or redistribution is strictly prohibited. All rights reserved.
This content is provided for test preparation purposes only and does not imply an endorsement by Mometrix of any particular political, scientific, or religious point of view.

At Recess — in the Ring —
We passed the Fields of Gazing Grain —
We passed the Setting Sun —

Or rather — He passed Us —
The Dews drew quivering and chill —
For only Gossamer, my Gown —
My Tippet — only Tulle —

We paused before a House that seemed
A Swelling of the Ground —
The Roof was scarcely visible —
The Cornice — in the Ground —

Since then — 'tis Centuries — and yet
Feels shorter than the Day
I first surmised the Horses' Heads
Were toward Eternity —

95. Which of the following best describes the tone of this poem?

a. Serious, grave, and portentously dark
b. Detached and alienated, with a numb, despairing feeling
c. Lighthearted, humorous, and gently ironic
d. Frantic and agitated, with a frenzy of fear

96. What is implicitly described in the fifth stanza?

a. A home
b. A grave
c. A church
d. A school

97. Throughout the poem, which of the following literary devices is used to describe death?

a. Analogy
b. Hyperbole
c. Alliteration
d. Personification

98. Within the literary genre of poetry, which function is more characteristic of the ballad than the sonnet?

a. Relating a story about human interactions
b. Demonstrating skill with writing the poem
c. Being included as part of theatrical plays
d. Satirizing romantic, political, and social issues

Copyright © Mometrix Media. You have been licensed one copy of this document for personal use only. Any other reproduction or redistribution is strictly prohibited. All rights reserved.
This content is provided for test preparation purposes only and does not imply an endorsement by Mometrix of any particular political, scientific, or religious point of view.

99. If an author of informational text makes a reference to someone famous, e.g., the name of a literary or historical figure, to create resonance with readers and/or make something or someone in the text symbolic, what rhetorical device is this?

a. Allusion
b. Paradox
c. Analogy
d. Parody

100. Of the following, which is NOT common in both satire and realism?

a. Irony
b. Serious tone
c. Exaggeration
d. Vernacular dialogue

101. "He woke up, looked at the clock, got dressed, ate a hurried breakfast, got into his car, drove downtown, parked the car, walked across the street and up the block to the corner building next to the grocery store, opened the front door, and went inside." What type of sentence is this?

a. Compound–complex
b. Compound sentence
c. A complex sentence
d. A simple sentence

102. Which of the following is true regarding choosing media for communicating ideas?

a. The budget available to the presenter is the sole influence.
b. When using mass media, a target audience is not relevant.
c. For social change, potential audience participation matters.
d. The duration of a message has no effect on media choices.

103. In a paired reading strategy for identifying the main idea in informational text, two students silently read a selection. Then, taking two-column notes of main ideas and supporting details, they take turns with the following steps. Which choice sequences these steps in the correct order?

a. The pair develops main idea consensus, a student paraphrases the main idea, a student explains agreement or disagreement, they take turns finding supporting details
b. A student paraphrases the main idea, a student explains agreement or disagreement, the pair develops main idea consensus, they take turns finding supporting details
c. They take turns finding supporting details, a student explains agreement or disagreement, a student paraphrases the main idea, the pair develops main idea consensus
d. A student explains agreement or disagreement, they take turns finding supporting details, the pair develops main idea consensus, a student paraphrases the main idea

Copyright © Mometrix Media. You have been licensed one copy of this document for personal use only. Any other reproduction or redistribution is strictly prohibited. All rights reserved.
This content is provided for test preparation purposes only and does not imply an endorsement by Mometrix of any particular political, scientific, or religious point of view.

104. A student writing a paper on a topic within a specialized discipline, which she has researched using textbooks published in that field, wants to make sure she has correctly spelled certain words that are part of the terminology peculiar to that discipline. Which reference should she best consult?

a. Spell checker
b. Style manual
c. Dictionary
d. Glossary

105. The first sentence of *The Bell Jar* by Sylvia Plath is as follows: "It was a queer, sultry summer, the summer they electrocuted the Rosenbergs, and I didn't know what I was doing in New York." What is most accurate about this sentence?

a. It establishes setting and character elements via literal meaning.
b. It establishes the symbols to be used throughout in an allegory.
c. It establishes the setting for a historical novel about the 1950s.
d. It establishes an extended metaphor using figurative meaning.

106. What is the purpose of an adverb in a sentence?

a. It identifies a person, place, or thing
b. It describes an action or state of being
c. It modifies a verb, adjective, or adverb
d. It describes or otherwise modifies a noun

107. In which of the following examples has the author created an instance of situational irony?

a. In *Great Expectations,* Pip and the readers think Miss Havisham is his benefactor, but it is Magwitch.
b. In *The Cask of Amontillado,* Fortunato says a cough won't kill him; Montresor replies, "True—true."
c. In *Romeo and Juliet,* Romeo, without the Friar's letter, thinks Juliet is dead; readers know she is alive.
d. In every one of these examples, the irony created is dramatic rather than verbal or situational irony.

108. Which author of young adult fiction won the Newbery Medal for her novel *A Wrinkle in Time*?

a. Lois Lowry
b. J. K. Rowling
c. Ursula K. Le Guin
d. Madeleine L'Engle

109. Which of the following was written by Mary Ann Evans under the *nom de plume* George Eliot?

a. *Emma*
b. *Agatha*
c. *Pride and Prejudice*
d. *Sense and Sensibility*

Copyright © Mometrix Media. You have been licensed one copy of this document for personal use only. Any other reproduction or redistribution is strictly prohibited. All rights reserved.
This content is provided for test preparation purposes only and does not imply an endorsement by Mometrix of any particular political, scientific, or religious point of view.

110. Which of the following statements is most accurate regarding passive voice as it relates to paragraph cohesion?

a. The passive voice makes paragraphs less cohesive.
b. The passive voice can be useful for paragraph cohesion.
c. The passive voice is critical for making paragraphs cohesive.
d. The passive voice should only be used when necessary.

Copyright © Mometrix Media. You have been licensed one copy of this document for personal use only. Any other reproduction or redistribution is strictly prohibited. All rights reserved.
This content is provided for test preparation purposes only and does not imply an endorsement by Mometrix of any particular political, scientific, or religious point of view.

Answer Key and Explanations for Test #1

Multiple Choice

1. B: The active reading strategy called text coding has nothing to do with writing computer code (a). Text monitoring is a synonym for text coding rather than a name for a different strategy (c). The authors cited recommend that, for students to perform text coding, teachers should model it for them (d) one or two codes at a time until students have learned all of the codes.

2. A: The thought behind this statement is most precisely described as a stereotype, so choice A is correct. A stereotype is an assumption or generalization made about everybody in an identified group. The other answer choices are accurate descriptions of the thought that the statement expresses; however, they are less precise. An inference (B) is a conclusion based on available evidence rather than a conclusion arrived at through logical deduction. The statement in question is not necessarily an inference, so choice B is incorrect. The statement does reflect an assumption (C), but there are many kinds of assumptions aside from stereotypes. Likewise, the statement is certainly a generalization (D), but generalizations can be made about anything, while this one pertains to a specific group of people, so it is more precisely described as a stereotype.

3. B: Choice B is correct because the stanza does not include paradox in any form. There are no contradictions in the stanza that are nevertheless true or profound. Choice A is incorrect because the stanza includes a simile, a comparison using *like* or *as*, in "Like geese about the sky." Choice C is incorrect because the stanza contains hyperbole, or an over-exaggeration for dramatic effect. It is an over-exaggeration, and possibly a metaphor, to say that one would love someone until the ocean is folded and hung up to dry. This is impossible and implies that the person will love forever. Choice D is incorrect because the stanza has an instance of alliteration, the use of repeated initial sounds in words, in "seven stars go squawking."

4. A: When evaluating the strength of an analysis that is based on textual evidence, we do not need to consider whether the analysis explains the author's intended meaning or purpose, so choice A is correct. The other choices are incorrect because they refer to considerations that are relevant when evaluating the strength of a prediction. Criteria for such an evaluation include standards for the evidence and standards for the analysis. The best possible evidence is strong (i.e., convincing), relevant, and accurate (B). Evidence should be specific, and it should be included in the analysis as a paraphrase or a direct quote (C). The best possible analysis shows special insight into a theme, character, or story event (D).

5. C: In inclusive educational programs, teachers must be willing to find solutions to their own needs through team-based problem-solving, so choice C is correct. Teachers must also meet not only student needs but the needs of students' families, so choice A is incorrect. Additionally, teachers should effectively communicate their own needs, so choice B is incorrect. They should meet these needs through team problem-solving, as mentioned in choice C, and not by seeking solutions independently, so choice D is incorrect.

6. B: Early ballad themes included jealousy, betrayal, murder, war, famine, poverty, etc. as well as love; early sonnet themes included politics, social standing, satire, etc. as well as love. Both genres have prominently featured expressions of love. The sonnet has five main kinds (A): the Petrarchan/Italian, Occitan, Shakespearean/English, Spenserian, and Modern; the ballad has developed many more variations in form. Originally the ballad was often set to music, and it was later associated with operas and musicals; the sonnet originated in dramatic plays and medieval

Copyright © Mometrix Media. You have been licensed one copy of this document for personal use only. Any other reproduction or redistribution is strictly prohibited. All rights reserved.
This content is provided for test preparation purposes only and does not imply an endorsement by Mometrix of any particular political, scientific, or religious point of view.

courts. Though some sonnets have been set to music, the sonnet did not originate with music (C). The standard ballad meter is iambic heptameter, albeit with variations; the standard sonnet meter is iambic pentameter (D).

7. C: Chopin's character development of Mrs. Mallard in the quotation includes repression and strength. These explain her not showing shock or denial but weeping immediately on hearing of her husband's apparent death, but also its short duration: "When the storm of grief had spent itself she went away to her room alone." The quotation does not explain her reaction to seeing her husband alive: identification of Louise's "heart trouble" in the first sentence helps explain her heart attack, along with character development indicating her relief at freedom from her husband's domination (despite his always loving her and her "sometimes" loving him). It does not explain his behavior: the paragraph describing his "powerful will bending hers" explains his controlling nature. The "joy" Chopin describes is NOT at seeing her husband alive, which kills her; Louise felt this joy previously upon believing he was dead ("free, free, free!").

8. C: The titles named are all epistolary novels, or novels told in the form of series of letters written by their characters. They are not picaresque novels, which tell the adventures of a roguish antihero (*pícaro* means "rogue" in Spanish) and are often humorous and/or satirical. Popular examples include Miguel de Cervantes' *Don Quixote*, Henry Fielding's *Joseph Andrews* and *Tom Jones*, and Charles Dickens' *Martin Chuzzlewit. The History of Emily Montague* by Frances Brooke (1769) was the first novel written in North America, as well as an epistolary novel, but the others were not first novels in their countries. Mary Shelley's *Frankenstein* (1818) was written in the 19th century; therefore, not all of these novels were written in the 18th century.

9. A: A slide show presentation is designed as a visual aid to summarize and highlight the main points in a speaker's talk. Slide show presentation slides commonly feature brief verbal phrases and sentences; are often numbered or bulleted; and also may include pictures, diagrams, graphs, and more. The slides not only visualize the speaker's main points for audiences, guide listeners through the presentation, and facilitate note-taking and outlining by listeners, they also help keep the speaker organized and on the subject. The slides provide an outline of the presentation; the speaker supplies the additional details. A poster is a visual aid, but not a technological tool. It would also not add as much to the presentation as a slide show. A blog and a wiki are both designed for audiences to read online, not to read while someone is speaking or to listen to someone reading them aloud.

10. D: No apostrophes are necessary in this sentence. Choice A is incorrect because possessive pronouns like *hers* and *theirs* do not use apostrophes like possessive nouns do (e.g., The book's pages). Choice B is incorrect because a family of people with the last name *Brown* would be referred to collectively as *the Browns* and not *the Brown's.* Choice C is incorrect because it contains the same errors as both choice A and choice B. Choice D correctly uses possessive pronouns and a plural proper noun.

11. D: The student has used the same adjective, "wonderful," four times in the same sentence to modify four different nouns. To give her description more variety, she should consult an online thesaurus to find synonyms (e.g., terrific, great, outstanding, exemplary, etc.). A grammar guide (a) will not offer vocabulary synonyms, and the student's sentence has no grammatical issues. An encyclopedia (b) offers information on many subjects, but not word synonyms. An online dictionary (c) will provide a few to several synonyms for "wonderful," but a thesaurus will offer many more.

12. C: Choice C is correct because *into small groups* is a prepositional phrase that modifies the phrasal verb *split up*. Choice A is incorrect because, even though *after* can be a preposition, in this case it is a subordinating conjunction because it is followed by a subject and a verb: *we arrive*.

Copyright © Mometrix Media. You have been licensed one copy of this document for personal use only. Any other reproduction or redistribution is strictly prohibited. All rights reserved.
This content is provided for test preparation purposes only and does not imply an endorsement by Mometrix of any particular political, scientific, or religious point of view.

Choice B includes *up*, which can often be a preposition, but in this case is an adverb that forms the phrasal verb *split up*. Choice D is an infinitive functioning as an adverb to show the purpose of the main verb phrase *will split up*.

13. C: Longer sentences are not necessarily clauses. A clause must have a subject and a finite verb. Choice C has no verb, so it is the correct answer. Choices A and B both contain clauses, so they are not correct. Choice D is also a clause, so it is incorrect. Note that it is possible to introduce a complete sentence with *then*, because it is an adverb, not a subordinating conjunction or a relative pronoun.

14. A: The first step a reader should take in evaluating the arguments in an informational text is to identify the conclusion the author draws with the argument. The second step is to identify what premises or reasons support this conclusion. The third step is to clarify these premises or reasons by paraphrasing them in the reader's own words, which can also show whether the premises fit with the conclusion they should support. The reader can then list all premises in order, followed by the conclusion, and note any assumptions or premises necessary to support the conclusion that the author may have omitted. The next step is judging whether a deductive reasoning argument is valid, or whether an inductive reasoning argument uses true premises that support the conclusion.

15. D: Outlines benefit students (A) and professional writers (B), not only one or the other. The main point(s) of a paragraph or an entire piece, and the details that support the main point(s), can be more quickly identified in outlines that summarize them in single sentences than they can by reading through all the additional language of a fully developed piece. Outlines can be used not only to plan writing (C), but also to analyze existing writing (D). Readers (or writers reviewing their own work) can make outlines to summarize the main point/idea in one sentence, and then list and number the supporting details, also each in a single sentence.

16. A: The introduction of an essay should get the reader's attention, engage the reader's interest, state and integrate the main thesis within it, and give an overview of the essay's organization or structure (for example, by summarizing the main point and supporting evidence). Developing the thesis statement and giving examples of the idea in the thesis both belong in the body of the essay. Giving the reader a sense of closure belongs in the conclusion of the essay.

17. B: Readers should first identify the conclusion of an argument and then identify the premises the author gives to support that conclusion. Choice A is incorrect because the reader cannot find support premises without knowing the conclusion that needs to be supported. Choice C is incorrect because the author may present supporting premises before their argument's conclusion, but readers should first identify the conclusion when evaluating arguments. Choice D is incorrect because readers should try to paraphrase the premises to clarify them and show how they support the conclusion.

18. B: Poems are the literary forms that most prominently use literary devices such as similes, metaphors, personification, etc. Although authors of plays (a); nonfiction (c) essays, books, etc.; and fictional short stories (d) may certainly use such devices (to varying extents depending on author purpose and style), those literary devices named are most prominently found in poems.

19. D: Research studies have shown that setting specific goals for writing promotes student motivation and sense of accomplishment. Developing student writing goals should not be a responsibility confined either to teachers or students: both teachers and students may develop writing goals, such as including more ideas within one paper, or incorporating specific elements of certain genres in compositions. Teachers and students may develop goals individually, in

Copyright © Mometrix Media. You have been licensed one copy of this document for personal use only. Any other reproduction or redistribution is strictly prohibited. All rights reserved.
This content is provided for test preparation purposes only and does not imply an endorsement by Mometrix of any particular political, scientific, or religious point of view.

collaboration, or both: students together, teachers together, and students with teachers—including individual students, student groups, individual teachers, and team/co-teachers.

20. D: The speaker's passivity and lack of control over the thought that inspires his or her writing can be interpreted from Ted Hughes's description of the thought as a fox that approaches unbidden, from outside, out of a blank nothingness. This passivity is emphasized by the description of the Thought-Fox as "Coming about its own business." Therefore, choice D is correct. The speaker as a passive recipient is further shown in the last stanza, where the fox "enters the dark hole of the head," and in the last line, "The page is printed." This also rules out that the writer guides the thought, so choice A is incorrect. Choice B is incorrect because the poem does not suggest that a writer must look to nature for inspiration, though the poem uses imagery and metaphor that involves nature. Choice C is incorrect because the fox represents the thought itself, rather than being a character or figure that assists the speaker in developing the thought or written work.

21. C: Author Ted Hughes uses extended metaphor by describing the concrete presence of a fox to represent the abstract concept of a writer's inspiration. From beyond the blank window, in the dark forest, the fox approaches like a thought comes to mind, leaving pawprints in the snow the way that a thought may lead to letters on a page. Because the entire poem is a metaphor, choice C is correct. Foreshadowing (A) is a literary device where the writer hints at something that will become more apparent later in a story. Though the poem includes the use of repetition (B), this is not the primary literary device used. Irony (D) is a literary device where the writer creates a noticeable difference between what is said in a story and what happens in it.

22. A: This poem was written in free verse, meaning it does not follow a metrical pattern, rhyme scheme, or particular poetic form, so choice A is correct. The poem is not in blank verse, which is poetry that follows a rhythm and metrical pattern but does not rhyme, so choice B is incorrect. Though the poem contains some rhymes, such as the eye rhyme of "snow" with "now," the slant rhyme of "star" with "near," and the rhyme of "snow" with "hollow," there is no regular rhyme scheme, so choice C is incorrect. The poem does not have a particular number of beats per line, so it is not metered, and choice D is incorrect.

23. B: The poem describes how the speaker is inspired to write, using the fox to embody a thought that enters the speaker's mind, hence the title "The Thought-Fox". It does not describe an actual fox or the process of observing one, so choice A is incorrect. Though the poem notes the ticking clock, it does not describe the process of merely passing the time, so choice C is incorrect. The poem describes the creative process and uses a metaphor from nature to do this, but it does not describe the specific process of creating from the inspiration of nature, so choice D is incorrect.

24. B: Of the choices given, the only one all three texts share in common is that a great flood was how each religion's god eliminated humans whose behavior had become wicked beyond any other remedy. In Genesis, the flood is described as occurring all over the world. However, the Quran describes the flood as regional (which is closer to fact according to historians and archeologists, who identify a tidal wave in the Middle East as the actual source of these narratives). Also, none of these texts describes everybody being destroyed by the flood: the Quran says Allah only destroys those who disregard his messengers' communications, and the Gilgamesh Epic and Genesis both include survivors. While the Gilgamesh Epic and Genesis tell of a man being instructed to build a ship to escape the flood, and the shipbuilder in both stories sends birds out after the flood to test its end, the Quran does not include the ship or birds.

25. A: Both groups of students most likely will find both texts conflict in their perspectives on the given topics. Lincoln opposed slavery, Douglas supported it; the two debated this topic while

Copyright © Mometrix Media. You have been licensed one copy of this document for personal use only. Any other reproduction or redistribution is strictly prohibited. All rights reserved.
This content is provided for test preparation purposes only and does not imply an endorsement by Mometrix of any particular political, scientific, or religious point of view.

running for president. The Romantic movement was an opposite reaction against the Enlightenment: the latter promoted rationalism, the former emotionalism. Their views of nature differed: Enlightenment thinkers sought to study it objectively, believing they could impose order; Romantics sought to celebrate its chaotic, complex potential, believing they could never completely understand or control it. Hence, both pairs would conflict, not one (b). They would unlikely be similar (c). Neither would differ only slightly (d).

26. A: Lack of parallelism. Corrections: "to stay at home, cook dinner, and *watch* TV" OR "*staying* at home, *cooking* dinner, and watching TV."

27. B: The first thing a researcher should look for in a review of the existing literature related to a specific research question is whether that question has already been definitively answered. If so, the researcher should ask a different research question. If the question has not already been answered conclusively, then the researcher can look for gaps in knowledge about the topic that searching the literature reveals; review the literature to find what needs and opportunities for further research other researchers have identified; examine the literature to discern whether there is consensus, controversy, or both; and if so, what those opinions are about the topic. These considerations help inform the direction for research.

28. B: Choice B is correct because differences among individual students are addressed very effectively by the diversity of formats and experiences available in digital media. Choice A is incorrect because the ability to navigate rapidly among various media is an advantage to all students and does not support individual differences. Choice C is similarly incorrect because the timeliness of updates in digital media are advantageous for all students. Choice D is incorrect because global access to information and people (such as experts, mentors, and peers) is, again, an advantage for every student and teacher.

29. C: Alcaeus, a lyrical poet of ancient (7th-6th century BC) Greece, was the first person known to use the metaphor of sailing a ship to represent the government of a city-state or republic. The playwright Aeschylus (6th-5th century BC), known for his tragedies (The Oresteia, Prometheus Bound), subsequently used this metaphor in his work Seven Against Thebes, also in ancient Greece. Thereafter another, very famous ancient Greek, philosopher and author Plato (5th-4th century BC) employed the same metaphor in his Republic. In the 19th century, English poet Henry Wadsworth Longfellow used the same figurative meaning as an extended metaphor throughout his 1850 poem, "O Ship of State." In 1865, Walt Whitman again used this extended metaphor in his poem "O Captain! My Captain!" an elegy on Lincoln's death.

30. D: Tracing and evaluating arguments and specific claims in a text are shared standards for grades 6 and 7, and delineating and evaluating arguments and specific claims in a text is a standard for grade 8 (a). Distinguishing whether claims are supported by evidence and reasons or not (b) is a part of the standard for grade 6 only. Assessing whether the reasoning in claims is sound and the evidence is relevant and sufficient to support the claims (c) is a part of the standards for grades 7 and 8. Recognizing whether irrelevant evidence has been introduced (d) is a part of the standard for grade 8 only.

31. B: Mood refers to the emotions evoked in the reader by the literary work, whereas tone refers to the emotions or attitude of the author toward the subject matter or audience, making choice B correct. Choice C is the reverse of this, so it is not correct. Choice A is incorrect because mood and tone do not mean the same thing. Though mood and tone have different meanings, neither one is associated with particular techniques; the same literary techniques could be used for either purpose, so choice D is incorrect.

Copyright © Mometrix Media. You have been licensed one copy of this document for personal use only. Any other reproduction or redistribution is strictly prohibited. All rights reserved.
This content is provided for test preparation purposes only and does not imply an endorsement by Mometrix of any particular political, scientific, or religious point of view.

32. B: Techniques promoting paragraph coherence include transitions (i.e., using words and phrases to connect ideas and sentences), repetition (i.e., repeating key words and phrases across sentences to reinforce their importance as well as help sentences flow together), parallelism (i.e., using adjacent phrases, clauses, or sentences that have the same syntax to make information easier to process), and consistency (i.e., making point of view, tone, register, voice, etc. uniform across a piece of writing). Since repetition is the only one of these that focuses on showing importance, choice B is correct, and the other choices are incorrect.

33. C: Choice C is correct, as research does not indicate any particular type of strategy is inherently more helpful than another. The other three choices broadly agree with research findings, so they are all incorrect. Multiple research studies have found that teaching cognitive strategies to students helps them with planning (B), composing, revising, and editing written compositions. Furthermore, research shows cognitive strategies for writing benefit students of all ages (A) and ability levels (D).

34. C: According to experts, research shows that teachers should explicitly teach their students writing strategies, including prewriting planning, composition, revision, and editing, by first modeling the strategies; then guiding students in practicing them; and then, once they have learned the strategies, letting students practice using them independently. They should not skip the guided practice step (A); students need assistance learning to apply demonstrated strategies before practicing on their own. Students learn better with, not without, teacher models (B), which must be presented before, not after, guided practice (D).

35. A: Bloggers need to use correct punctuation to encourage continued reading of their posts. If they are not already confident in their grasp of punctuation, they should write in shorter sentences until they are. Because reading on computer screens is harder than on paper, paragraphs in blogs must be significantly shorter than in print, not longer. Shorter paragraphs enable readers to "chunk" the information. Font sizes should be larger rather than smaller to be easier on readers' eyes and more legible onscreen.

36. C: The clauses in the sentence are as follows: *Because he was late* is a dependent clause because it is introduced by the subordinating conjunction *because* and therefore cannot stand alone; *he missed the field trip* is an independent clause because it can stand alone as a sentence; *and this caused him to fail the class* is also an independent clause. Since there are two independent clauses and one dependent clause, choice C is correct, and the other choices are incorrect.

37. B: This stanza is an example of hyperbole (B), showing how extreme something is by exaggerating to an impossible degree. W. H. Auden describes things that will never happen to emphasize the extent of the speaker's love. Hubris (A) means excessive pride, defined in ancient Greek literature and later continued by Shakespeare and many other authors as a tragic flaw. A hyperbaton (C) is the inversion of conventional word order (e.g. "Away he walked" instead of "He walked away"). Hypophora (D) is when a character asks a question and immediately answers it (e.g., "Did you just do that? You just did that.").

38. C: Choice C is correct because both TV and radio can raise awareness, interest, and excitement. Choice A is incorrect because both TV and radio are high-status mass media (i.e., they reach many people). Choice B is incorrect, as TV has a broad reach and radio has a broad-to-medium reach. Choice D is incorrect because, while TV enables messages to be targeted for certain audiences, radio works better for specific audiences, such as people who listen to a particular local station every day.

39. B: Informal assessments can consist of everyday activities, such as grading homework, observing students, taking anecdotal records, and talking to students about their learning.

Copyright © Mometrix Media. You have been licensed one copy of this document for personal use only. Any other reproduction or redistribution is strictly prohibited. All rights reserved.
This content is provided for test preparation purposes only and does not imply an endorsement by Mometrix of any particular political, scientific, or religious point of view.

Therefore, the results are not standardized, making it difficult to compare results among groups or over time. The other options describe limitations of formal assessments, which may increase student anxiety and can be more expensive and time consuming to implement and score.

40. A: Blogs (short for "web logs") are published online, where anybody with Internet access may read them. Bloggers may post occasionally, monthly, weekly, daily, or whenever they want. It is not uncommon for bloggers to post weekly or daily. Journals are more typical for private entries, similar to diaries. People often make journal entries daily or less often, similarly to blog posts but less publicly. (Some people also publish journals—in print or online as collections in books or e-books, or as ongoing online publications similar to blogs. However, journal writing is more often private, whereas blogging never is.) Letters are typically to others, not private (except for therapeutic letters written to vent emotions but never sent); and though sometimes published online (such as letters to the editor, open letters, or newsletters, among others), usually not daily. Essays are typically not written daily and privately or published online. Speeches are typically written for oral delivery, not daily online publication or as private activities.

41. D: Mobile and text media are very popular (a) and increasingly so, an advantage for effective public communications. Another advantage of text messaging using mobile phones is the timeliness (b) with which information and reminders can be sent. Especially for public communications intended to effect social change, their interactive (c) potential is an additional advantage. Other advantages include decreasing costs and increasing rural reach. One disadvantage of this media format is the limited length (d) to which messages are restricted. However, most presenters work around this disadvantage by inserting hyperlinks to websites/webpages for accessing further information. Other disadvantages include provider charges, although today, more providers are including free texting in mobile plans.

42. A: News articles published on the internet are more formal in their content and language than blogs (B), which are written from a more personal, less journalistic perspective. News articles are also more formal than emails (C), which can be even more casual than blogs as they involve communications between individuals rather than writing intended for larger audiences like blogs and news articles. Hence, these are not all the same in formality level (D).

43. A: In the organization stage of writing, the writer determines the purpose, thesis, and supporting details of the written work. In other words, the organization stage is the part of the writing process where the writer decides on the structure of the proposed written work. In this stage, the writer organizes the ideas already decided upon in the prewriting stage.

44. C: The meaning of this opening sentence is primarily literal: it establishes who the main character is, what he does, and his current situation. While this novella contains some symbols, the opening sentence is not symbolic (a) of anything particular. The meaning is not implicit (b) but explicit. (Hemingway was known for the clear, direct simplicity of his writing style.) The sentence is not true (d) because this book is a work of fiction.

45. C: An informational text that explains one or more problems and how to solve those problems would follow a problem-solution text structure, so choice C is the correct answer. A process narrative structure would lay out a sequence of steps or stages. This structure would be more fitting for an informational text about how to write an essay rather than how to avoid errors commonly found in essays, so choice A is not the correct answer. Cause-and-effect structure organizes writing by whether the events being described are causes or effects. According to the question, the informational text would include some description of the effects of common writing mistakes. However, the whole text would not be organized based on these, so choice B is incorrect.

Copyright © Mometrix Media. You have been licensed one copy of this document for personal use only. Any other reproduction or redistribution is strictly prohibited. All rights reserved.
This content is provided for test preparation purposes only and does not imply an endorsement by Mometrix of any particular political, scientific, or religious point of view.

Finally, a description uses sensory language, such as imagery, to help readers experience the subject of the writing. This structure would not be useful in listing common errors found in essays nor in explaining how to avoid these errors, so choice D is incorrect.

46. C: To get data to inform a school improvement plan (a), a teacher could use a summative assessment, comparing student scores at the end of the school year to their baseline scores obtained at the beginning of that year. This can also be done to show accountability to the federal government (e.g., meeting adequate yearly progress criteria) to get or keep school funding (b); and to get data on student progress toward instructional objectives over the entire school year (d). A teacher would use a formative assessment to get data about individual student performance (c); summative assessments yield more group data and less individual data.

47. B: This is an example of a metaphor. The literal meaning of hemorrhaging is copious bleeding. In this example it is used figuratively in a metaphor for losing money at a volume and rate comparable to severe blood loss denoted by hemorrhage. It is not a generalization. An example of using a generalization persuasively is "We all want peace, not war." It is not a rhetorical question or a question at all. An example of using a rhetorical question (needing no answer) persuasively is "Wouldn't you rather get paid more than less?" The example is not of negative connotation, because the word "hemorrhage" already has a negative denotation—in other words, the literal meaning of hemorrhaging is never a good thing. An example of using negative word connotation persuasively is, "You could stay with this *expensive* plan..." followed by contrasting positive connotation: "...or choose the *money-saving* plan I'm offering."

48. B: Choice B is correct because dialogue can be used to bring themes and meanings into clearer focus and change the course of the plot. Choice A is incorrect because dialogue can be used to advance the plot and to develop characters. Choice C is incorrect because dialogue should not be used merely to break up exposition, and it does not by itself slow the pace of the story. Choice D is incorrect because dialogue can be used to reproduce real-life speech patterns and to add drama to a story.

49. C: This is an example of a slippery slope argument that is a logical fallacy. The fallacious form of the slippery slope is essentially a non sequitur—it argues that one thing will cause other things without showing any cause-and-effect relationship between them. A straw man argument is a logical fallacy which, instead of refuting someone else's actual argument, refutes an exaggeration or caricature of it. A red herring is a piece of irrelevant information introduced to distract attention from the real issue. *Post hoc ergo propter hoc* is Latin for "After this, therefore because of this." It means arguing that one thing was caused by another that happened before it. This is a logical fallacy because, like correlation, chronological order does not equal causation.

50. D: Choice D is correct because it reflects a ground rule that only warrants mention for younger children and children with behavioral disorders. The rule prohibits physically aggressive behaviors that are not common among older, typically developing children. The other choices are incorrect because they show rules that students' attention must be drawn to regardless of age or developmental level. These include no cross-talk (A), no interrupting others (B), and no monopolizing the discussion (C).

51. C: Evidence-based instructional approaches are proven via multiple rigorous research studies sharing consistent results. Choice C is correct because student outcomes should be evaluated using appropriate, established measures. Choice A is incorrect because the teaching practices should be defined in advance in order to evaluate the effectiveness of approaches. Choice B is incorrect because evaluators should establish a monitoring process to assure compliance. Choice D is

Copyright © Mometrix Media. You have been licensed one copy of this document for personal use only. Any other reproduction or redistribution is strictly prohibited. All rights reserved.
This content is provided for test preparation purposes only and does not imply an endorsement by Mometrix of any particular political, scientific, or religious point of view.

incorrect because student progress with a specific teaching method should be compared to their progress without that method via suitable means.

52. C: Choice C is correct because journaling can be a form of free writing, which serves to develop writing skills. Choice A is incorrect as many journals are written for documentation or autobiographical purposes, and many authors write journals they expect or hope to publish someday. Choice B is incorrect because journals are not confined to any particular form or structure. Choice D is incorrect because journaling is often used for its therapeutic benefits for the writer.

53. A: The sentence in choice A uses two metaphors: "He became a tiger" and "he turned into a pussycat." These give readers a better understanding of the person being discussed by comparing his qualities, characteristics, and behaviors to those of more familiar examples—in this case, tigers and domestic cats. Metaphors explicitly state one thing is another, while similes use "like" or "as" to make comparisons. Although similes are also considered figurative language, they are not metaphors, making choice B incorrect. Choices C and D are incorrect because both of these sentences are literal.

54. C: An effective teacher technique for meeting learning goals in classroom discussions if students get off the subject is to restate the topics and questions they previously stated. Another good redirection technique is to ask new questions about the same topics. To encourage creative and varied student responses, teachers should ask questions instead of making comments, not vice versa. Teachers making comments discourages students from doing the same, whereas asking questions invites them to offer different feedback. When some students dominate the discussion, a technique whereby teachers can engage more reticent students is to ask less challenging questions, not more: less challenging questions can be answered by any student, even unprepared ones. A checklist based on the class attendance roll is a good way to assess whether all students are participating.

55. C: Literacy skills are various and include a number of different sub-skills: reading fluency, comprehension, application of knowledge, listening, speaking, grammar, spelling, writing, and more. It is important for teachers to track student development for lesson design and to communicate with the student, future teachers, and parents. Therefore, it is best to keep samples of a variety of assessments, including descriptions of reading fluency, writing samples, projects, and formal assessments of grammar, spelling, and other skills. All of these skills develop simultaneously, but at different rates. Therefore, it is impossible to judge a student's literacy based only on one measure of assessment.

56. A: In classrooms based on differentiated instruction, the most common differentiation is the way in which individual students access the content they learn, as individual student differences often dictate differential means of access. It is common for learning goals to be assessed by standardized testing, which is not differentiated as often except when individual students require alternative assessment. All students in the differentiated classroom should be taught the same concepts. The only differentiation is the level of complexity at which concepts are taught, which is individualized. Instructional concepts should not be detailed, but broad and generalized for all students to acquire the same principles and skills.

57. A: Departing from Aristotle's ancient Greek definitions, later aestheticians have defined the poetic genres of epic (sometimes referred to as narrative), lyric, and dramatic, so choice A is correct, and the other choices are incorrect. Contrary to Aristotle's definition of lyric poetry (which included being sung, being accompanied by a lyre, and having a specific meter), lyric poetry has a

Copyright © Mometrix Media. You have been licensed one copy of this document for personal use only. Any other reproduction or redistribution is strictly prohibited. All rights reserved.
This content is provided for test preparation purposes only and does not imply an endorsement by Mometrix of any particular political, scientific, or religious point of view.

contemporary definition as poetry that expresses feelings. Epic and dramatic poetry have largely retained their definitions. Meanwhile, comic poetry and tragic poetry have come to be considered subgenres of dramatic poetry.

58. D: Relating stories of fictional characters is not a typical purpose of journal writing, so choice D is correct. Although a narrative may be written in the form of journal entries that are imagined to be written by a character in the narrative, such writing is still narrative writing, and not genuine journaling. The other choices each refer to a common purpose of journal writing. Each of these three options are generally introspective subjects someone might write about so they can remember it in more detail later or keep track of how far they have come.

59. A: This version is correctly punctuated because it is a compound-complex sentence, consisting of two independent clauses and a dependent/subordinate (relative) clause. Independent clauses should be separated by a semicolon. In (B) and (D), the two independent clauses have no punctuation separating them, creating a run-on sentence; additionally, (B) has an incorrect comma between the first independent clause and the subordinating conjunction "that," which introduces the relative clause. (If "that" were omitted, it would be correct with or without the comma.) Version (C) incorrectly separates the independent clauses with a comma instead of a semicolon.

60. D: In the active reading strategy of text coding or text monitoring, students write preset codes to note their comprehension status in the margins of the text or on sticky notes, so choice D is correct. Choice A is incorrect as text coding does not involve students separating codes into columns—a technique used in the two-column notes reading strategy. Choice B is incorrect because text coding may involve writing codes, instead of main points, on sticky notes. Choice C is incorrect as text coding does not involve summarizing a text.

61. A: Choice A is correct because this sentence is an example of a compound-complex structure, which combines two independent clauses with one or more dependent clauses. *Bess loves art* is an independent clause, and it is modified by the relative clause (a type of dependent clause), *who can draw beautifully*. *Grace prefers science* is also an independent clause, and it is modified by another relative clause, *who thinks very logically*. The two independent clauses are joined by the conjunction *but*. The other choices are not correct, as they refer to the other three sentence structures. A compound sentence has two independent clauses but no dependent clauses. A complex sentence has one independent and one dependent clause. A simple sentence is one independent clause.

62. D: With digital media, teachers and students alike can use cross-media transformations to convert speech to text and text to speech, including automatically by embedding speech-to-text and text-to-speech software into browsers and other software programs. Choices A, B, and C are all advantages for diverse students that can be accomplished using HTML and/or XML to change or select fonts and make similar text choices.

63. B: The word *first* shows that this sentence describes the beginning of Maria's family's process for planning holiday celebrations. This is an appropriate detail to follow Maria's introductory sentence. Choices A and C are not clearly relevant to the topic sentence. While these may be important details later, neither of these sentences should follow the topic sentence. Choice D should be included later in the composition, as the word *afterwards* shows that the described step occurs later.

64. A: *–tion* is a suffix because it comes at the end of a word. It turns a verb into a noun: *attend* becomes *attention, convert* becomes *conversion, present-presentation, converse-conversation, ambulate-ambulation,* and more. Prefixes, suffixes, and infixes are all affixes. However, *-tion* does

Copyright © Mometrix Media. You have been licensed one copy of this document for personal use only. Any other reproduction or redistribution is strictly prohibited. All rights reserved.
This content is provided for test preparation purposes only and does not imply an endorsement by Mometrix of any particular political, scientific, or religious point of view.

not turn nouns into pronouns. Pronouns are *I, me, we, us, you, he, she, they, them, it* (personal pronouns); *this, that, these, those, such* (demonstrative pronouns); *who, whom, which, that* (relative pronouns); *somebody, anybody, everybody, each, every, all, some, none, one* (indefinite pronouns); *myself, ourselves, yourself, himself, herself, themselves* (intensive or reflexive pronouns); and many more. The *-tion* suffix does not come at beginnings of words and hence is not a prefix, and does not make nouns into verbs—such as *fright* into *frighten*—but vice versa. Infixes come in the middles of words, like *s* in *mothers-in-law* or *passers-by*; or in expressions like "abso-blooming-lutely" in *My Fair Lady. -tion* is not an infix and does not make a noun into an adjective, such as *danger* into *dangerous.*

65. A: When a person argues against a proposition on the grounds that it will lead to a chain of similar events that will have an undesirable outcome, they are using the slippery slope fallacy. In the example given, the person opposes the legalization of one drug on the grounds that more and more drugs will inevitably be legalized as a consequence. It cannot be assumed that these other legalizations will take place simply because of this one, so the person is using the slippery slope fallacy, and choice A is correct. The other choices are incorrect because they refer to fallacies that are not being used here. A non sequitur (B) involves a conclusion that is not logically connected to a suggested cause (e.g., "He is rich, so he must be happy"). A red herring (C) introduces irrelevant information to distract attention from the actual issue. A straw man (D) misrepresents the opposing argument and then refutes the misrepresentation rather than the real argument.

66. C: Dante Alighieri's *Divine Comedy* (*Inferno*, *Purgatorio*, and *Paradiso*) (a) is an epic poem and a religious allegory. John Milton's *Paradise Lost* (b) is also an epic poem and religious allegory, and so is Edmund Spenser's *The Faerie Queene* (d). However, James Joyce's *Ulysses* (c) is a novel, not a poem. Though Joyce wanted this novel to be an epic, modeled its chapters on adventures of Ulysses (Odysseus) in Homer's epic poem the *Odyssey,* and drew parallels between his characters and Homer's, this book is nevertheless a Modernist novel with elements of realism rather than an epic poem.

67. C: This is an example of a dangling participle. The participle *completing* was done by Peter, but the sentence construction makes it seem as if the teacher did it. This makes no sense: the teacher would not give Peter a high grade after completing the assignment correctly. It can be corrected to "After Peter completed the assignment correctly, the teacher gave him a high grade" or "After completing the assignment correctly, Peter received a high grade from the teacher."

68. C: "Although we liked Bill and Hillary" is a dependent clause. It is a clause because it has a subject, "we," and a verb, "liked." It is dependent, or subordinate, because it begins with a subordinating conjunction, "although." So it cannot stand alone as an independent clause, but depends on and modifies the independent clause "we did not go (to their party)." It is not a prepositional phrase as it does not begin with a preposition. It is not a complete sentence because it is not an independent clause.

69. B: Three nouns are included in the compound subject of this sentence, so the verb should be the plural "are," not the singular "is." There is only one verb, so any error of agreement between/among verb tenses (C) is impossible. Lack of parallel structure (D) involves disagreement among grammatical structures, e.g., "walking, running, and to jump" instead of "walking, running, and jumping." There is no such error in this sentence. Because (B) is correct, (A) is incorrect.

70. B: *Activating* is the term experts use to identify the reading strategy whereby the reader activates prior knowledge and applies it to the new information in reading to construct meaning from it. *Inferring* is a strategy whereby the reader combines what the text states explicitly with

Copyright © Mometrix Media. You have been licensed one copy of this document for personal use only. Any other reproduction or redistribution is strictly prohibited. All rights reserved.
This content is provided for test preparation purposes only and does not imply an endorsement by Mometrix of any particular political, scientific, or religious point of view.

what it does not state but implies, and combines these both with what s/he already knows to draw inferences. *Questioning* is the reading strategy whereby the reader engages in "learning dialogues" with the text, author, classmates, and teachers to ask and answer questions about the text. *Summarizing* is the reading strategy whereby the reader paraphrases or restates what s/he perceives as the text's meaning.

71. B: Shakespeare used the connotative meanings of the words to create a metaphor, wherein the stage, players, exits and entrances, and parts played symbolize the world, people, and roles or stages in life. Therefore, his meaning is NOT primarily denotative (a), i.e., focusing on the literal word definitions; nor is it half denotative and half connotative (c). The words must have one or the other type of meaning, not neither (d): text authors use words literally or figuratively or both.

72. B: The author wants readers to infer that the narrator is indeed mad—not only because the narrator repeatedly and strenuously denies that he is, but also because he brags about the careful planning involved in committing a murder. In addition, the narrator seems to believe that this clever planning is proof of his sanity, but this belief only confirms that he does not see his own irrationality. Choice A is the opposite inference. Choices C and D, while arguably true, are not inferences that the author wants readers to make.

73. A: A primary characteristic of informative or explanatory writing is that the author assumes certain facts or truths, as informative writing is an attempt to work from existing knowledge in order to convey new knowledge. Therefore, choice A is correct. Choice B is incorrect because descriptive writing does not rely as heavily on assumed truths. Instead, descriptive writing uses sensory details to allow readers to experience what is being described. Choice C is incorrect because persuasive writing endeavors to convince readers of a truth. Choice D is incorrect because narrative writing relates a story to readers and does not depend on facts.

74. B: When students work in pairs to read and identify parts of an informational text to aid their comprehension, they read portions silently, discuss and agree on what they believe to be the main idea, and then identify details that would support that idea. This process is best summarized by choice B, so it is the correct answer. Identifying genres is not always necessary for comprehension, so choice A is incorrect. While prior knowledge is a consideration in the reading of informational text, a paired reading exercise to aid in comprehension need not involve the students identifying their shared prior knowledge, so choice C is incorrect. Identifying external texts that support the author's view may be necessary as part of research for a paper, but it is not necessary for understanding an informational text, so choice D is incorrect.

75. B: Miss Havisham uses Estella, not vice versa (a), by raising her to break men's hearts to gain revenge against men for her fiancé having left her at the altar. Estella in turn marries Drummle to get revenge on Miss Havisham (b) for using her. Magwitch uses Pip by raising Pip's social status to get revenge against society, not Pip (c), for discriminating against Magwitch in court on the basis of social class. Orlick wants revenge against Pip, not vice versa (d), for a series of wrongs he feels Pip committed and for Pip's privileged life, which Orlick envies.

76. A: When hasty generalization is used as a method of appeal, the author uses anecdotal or insufficient evidence to make generalizations about ideas or people that are not fully based in fact. They may be based on anecdotal evidence (e.g., "my neighbor smoked a pack of cigarettes a day and lived to be one hundred, so cigarettes must not be unhealthy") or can be based on evidence from small sample sizes or non-representative samples and extrapolated to the population as a whole (e.g., "Johnson is currently winning the presidential election in Smith County, so he will be the next president"). Rhetorical questions force agreement by asking a question that most people would

Copyright © Mometrix Media. You have been licensed one copy of this document for personal use only. Any other reproduction or redistribution is strictly prohibited. All rights reserved.
This content is provided for test preparation purposes only and does not imply an endorsement by Mometrix of any particular political, scientific, or religious point of view.

answer the same way (e.g., "Wouldn't you rather be paid more than less?"). Transfer and association persuades through the associating of one idea with something or someone that the audience is likely to agree with (e.g., advertising products by showing them being used by popular public figures). Ad hominem attacks occur when the author attacks the person giving the argument rather than the argument itself (e.g., "My opponent failed calculus when he was in college. We should not listen to someone who is bad at math!").

77. A: Toni Morrison's novels focus on black women and their search for a place within American culture and society. She often uses fantasy to explore the themes of racism, gender bias, and class conflict. She is both a Nobel Prize and Pulitzer Prize winner. Her novels include *The Bluest Eye, Sula, Song of Solomon*, and *Beloved.*

78. C: Only choice C accurately describes a criterion for evaluating the credibility of a website as an information source. When viewing a website, it is necessary to watch for writer and publisher bias, as the writer and anyone with a stake in the success of the website may have their own agendas. Choice A is incorrect because the domain name of a website and the publisher of a website are both important to consider. Likewise, choice B is incorrect because whether the information on a website can be corroborated and how recently it has been updated are both important considerations for an online source's credibility. Choice D is incorrect because links to, citations of, and recommendations for other sources generally add credibility, particularly if the other sources are reliable or authoritative.

79. A: Considering audience is not necessary in order to determine purpose, so choice A is correct. Choice B is incorrect because writers should use audience and purpose to decide on the best structure and organization for those who will read the writing. Choice C is incorrect, as audience, along with purpose of writing, will determine what style and tone to use in a piece of writing, and will therefore affect word choice. Identifying an audience will also help in choosing specific words that will be most understandable and appealing to readers. Finally, choice D is incorrect because audience will also dictate how much time to spend on research. Some readers will expect more supporting evidence, while others will not.

80. D: Reporting case studies is the best example of using rhetoric to provide supporting evidence of an author's main point in an informational text. Writing evocative descriptions is an example of using rhetoric to appeal to the reader's emotions in an informational text, not to provide supporting evidence. Making good analogies is an example of using rhetoric to illustrate and/or illuminate the author's point(s) rather than actually supporting them with evidence. Telling personal anecdotes is an example of using rhetoric to give readers examples that are more accessible and realistic to illustrate their points, rather than to provide evidence supporting them.

81. D: The evaluator of a summary of a literary passage should consider whether the student's summary achieves an equal balance of concision and completeness, so (A) is incorrect. The student should also summarize the passage objectively and neutrally, excluding their own reactions or opinions, so (B) is incorrect. The summary should cover the passage's points in a similar proportion as the original text, so (C) is incorrect. Finally, the student should tag attributions of ideas to their original authors by name, cite the passage's original source so summary readers can find it, and avoid overusing quotations. This means (D) is the correct answer.

82. C: Denotation is the literal meaning or dictionary definition of a word. Connotation is the figurative meaning of a word, including emotional or perceptual associations associated with the word but not included in its literal definition. The words "politician" and "statesman" have the same

Copyright © Mometrix Media. You have been licensed one copy of this document for personal use only. Any other reproduction or redistribution is strictly prohibited. All rights reserved.
This content is provided for test preparation purposes only and does not imply an endorsement by Mometrix of any particular political, scientific, or religious point of view.

literal meaning or denotation. However, when used in context, "politician" may have either a neutral or negative connotation, whereas "statesman" usually has a positive connotation.

83. C: This is a complex sentence. It has one independent clause ("He could not finish the test in time") and a dependent clause ("even though he tried his hardest"), which is subordinate to and depends on the independent clause. It is not a compound–complex (A) sentence, which would have two independent clauses and at least one dependent clause, because it has only one independent clause. It is not a compound (B) sentence, which has at least two independent clauses but no dependent clauses, because it has only one independent clause and does include a dependent clause. It is not a simple (D) sentence, which would be only one independent clause with no dependent clause.

84. B: Satire is a genre of writing that may be used in informational as well as literary (and informational literary) texts to ridicule human and social faults through various indirect devices, including irony (A), i.e., saying the opposite of what one means; overstatement (C), i.e., exaggerating; and/or understatement (D), i.e., minimizing the importance or seriousness of something in describing it.

85. D: Writers of technical language, as in scientific informational texts, need to find a balance between seeming too self-deprecating or too grandiose. For example, "our findings will change the world" is grandiose, whereas "our findings are insignificant" is self-deprecating. "Our results are promising and indicate the need for further research" is more balanced. These are examples of the mood of the language. Technical language should be concise by not using superfluous words, impersonal and detached by using passive voice and avoiding overuse of the first person and the vernacular, and professional by using more technical terminology rather than more familiar everyday vocabulary. These are examples of the tone of the language.

86. B: Students should always target an audience, perform an audience analysis, and develop an audience profile to determine what they should include in or omit from their writing. Even though the assigning teacher may be the only one to read the writing, students still need to identify an audience (A) and should not write as if the teacher is the main audience (D). In addition to knowing their purpose for writing before beginning, students should also consider what purpose their writing will meet for their readers (C) and how it is likely to be used.

87. B: The primary purpose of visual aids is to extend or enhance meaning. Visuals can sometimes distract from the meaning of the presentation if used too much, as in Choice A. Choice C could also create distractions in that students may be more likely to look at photos directly in front of them than pay attention to the student presenting. The final choice simply encourages students to read the information on screen, and will likely cause the presenting student to read aloud rather than communicate in his own words. Choice B, however, utilizes the students' thought processes in determining where a visual might help enhance understanding, and requires them to use oral communication as well.

88. C: Although both subgenres are fiction, they are not always about fictional *characters* (a): some tell fictional *stories* about *real* characters—e.g., Anthony Burgess's novel *Nothing Like the Sun* about what he imagined as Shakespeare's life, or Mary Renault's *The Bull from the Sea* about her conception of Theseus (apparently historical figure and myth combined) and the Minotaur. Similarly, other historical and science fiction may contain only fictional characters' fictional individual experiences, but within actual events—e.g., Esther Forbes' novel *Johnny Tremain*, set before and during the American Revolution. Thomas Pynchon's historical novel *Against the Day*; science fiction novels *Earth* by David Brin, *Callahan's Key* by Spider Robinson, *The Astronauts* by

Copyright © Mometrix Media. You have been licensed one copy of this document for personal use only. Any other reproduction or redistribution is strictly prohibited. All rights reserved.
This content is provided for test preparation purposes only and does not imply an endorsement by Mometrix of any particular political, scientific, or religious point of view.

Stanislaw Lem; and many others were based on a 1908 explosion (probably from a meteorite or comet) in Tunguska, Siberia. Numerous other examples exist. Some historical and science fiction works are closely aligned with facts; others are far more imaginative (d). Because they are ultimately fiction, both involve some kind of speculation (c).

89. A: The comma that is located before "his Idylls of the King" represents a comma splice and should be replaced with a period, a semicolon, or a comma and a coordinating conjunction. The two statements before and after the comma represent individual sentences and cannot be joined with a comma alone.

90. B: When an informational text author does not explicitly state their point of view or purpose, the reader should determine this themselves by asking certain questions. Evaluating the effectiveness of the author's choice and use of evidence is not helpful for determining author point of view or purpose, so choice B is correct. There are four considerations the reader can make in order to determine the author's point of view or purpose: what the author wants to accomplish by writing the text (A), what the author wants to persuade readers to agree with or believe (C), how the author's word choice affects the reader's perceptions of the subject matter (D), and how the author's choices of examples or facts affect the reader's perceptions of the subject matter.

91. D: To evaluate source credibility, researchers consider not only an author's reputation in the field, but equally whether s/he cites sources. These two commonly (but not always) go hand-in-hand: generally, authors respected in their fields are responsible and cite sources. (In popular fields, some individuals gain favorable reputations without responsible scholarship. This is less common in rigorous academic fields.) In some rapidly changing fields, for instance information technologies, sources must be current; in others, such as 19th-century American history (barring new historical discoveries), information published decades ago may still be accurate. Researchers must consider author point of view and purpose, which affect neutrality. Sources from certain points of view can be credible, but may restrict subject treatment to one side of a debate. Audience values influence what they consider credible: younger readers accept Internet sources more, academics value refereed journals, and local community residents may value mainstream sources like *Newsweek* magazine.

92. C: William Shakespeare's plays are good literary examples of poetry within fictional drama because they are written in verse form. Poems typically do not contain inserted prose (A). Plays are not generally known to incorporate pieces of fictional prose (B). Nonfictional prose sometimes incorporates quotations of poetry or even occasionally original poems, but this occurs much less often than with Shakespeare's plays and many others written entirely or mostly in poetry (D).

93. B: Teachers should base rubrics on their identified lesson objectives. They should explain a rubric to students in advance, and have students refer to the rubric as a guide while they work. Teachers should then use the rubric to assess whether students have met all included learning objectives. Rubrics can be used as both formative and summative assessment tools, meaning they were assessed either during or after the work, respectively. Rubrics are not replacements for clearly stating learning goals, objectives, expectations, and teacher modeling of expected performance: teachers should do all of these to enable optimal student performance, as well as supply a rubric to guide and assess student work. Teachers should also make very clear to students the relationship between learning goals and their performance.

94. C: Throughout this epic poem, Henry Wadsworth Longfellow employs trochaic tetrameter (a trochee is /∪, i.e., two syllables, the first stressed, the second unstressed; tetrameter is four beats per line) to evoke for his readers the rhythms of the Native Americans' chanting. Though he asks

Copyright © Mometrix Media. You have been licensed one copy of this document for personal use only. Any other reproduction or redistribution is strictly prohibited. All rights reserved.
This content is provided for test preparation purposes only and does not imply an endorsement by Mometrix of any particular political, scientific, or religious point of view.

and answers a series of questions in his Introduction, Longfellow never uses couplets (A), (B); the stanzas vary in length, but are all longer than two lines each. He does not use irony to develop a theme (D).

95. C: While the topic of this poem is death, the tone is lighthearted, and the poem finds humor in death with a gentle kind of irony, so choice C is correct. The diction, word choice, rhythms, and conclusion do not convey gravity or darkness (A). The descriptive details of the journey to eternity, slow yet seemingly over within a day in retrospect, do not convey detachment, alienation, or numbness (B). Rather, the persona in the poem seems to go on a pleasant journey with death and quietly observes Death's "kindly" character and "Civility"—examples of the gentle irony that the poet uses here. The deliberate, placid narrative has no frantic, agitated, frenzied, or fearful (D) qualities.

96. B: The fifth stanza, about "a House that seemed/A Swelling of the Ground," is an oblique description of a grave. Its cornice is "in the Ground" and the roof is "scarcely visible," indicating that this "House" is underground. This is not a literal description of a home (A) or a church (C). A school (D) with children at recess is described as one of the aspects of life they pass in their journey, in the third stanza. The fifth stanza's description of a grave is in keeping with the whole poem's light, gentle, indirect, and accepting treatment of death.

97. D: The author of this poem, Emily Dickinson, uses personification by attributing human qualities to nonhuman entities. She describes how Death "kindly stopped for me" and "knew no haste." She also uses human pronouns, such as "He" and "We," and human actions, such as "drove," "knew," and "paused." The poem's speaker even sets aside their "labor and [their] leisure too" to be polite to death. Analogy (A) is a comparison of different things that have some common attribute, like saying that the human heart is like a pump. The poem does analogize (for example, by describing a house that is really a grave), but the poem as a whole describes death using personification. Hyperbole (B) is extreme exaggeration, which there is no use of here. Alliteration (C) is repetition of sounds in adjacent or close words. Although the poem contains some uses of alliteration, such as "Gazing Grain" and "Setting Sun," the overall description of death uses personification.

98. A: One major defining characteristic of the ballad is its narrative function. Traditional ballads tell stories of love, jealousy, revenge, murder, etc.; broadside ballads were composed to entertain and inform the common people about current events; literary ballads enabled intellectuals and the socially elite to express themselves artistically. Historical functions of the sonnet include demonstrating one's skill writing in a highly structured poetic form (b); being featured prominently in theatrical plays (c) (some early plays included ballads, but not to the extent of sonnets); and satirizing romantic, political, and social issues of the time (d).

99. A: An allusion is a reference to something or someone well-known that adds symbolism and/or resonance. A paradox (B) is a seemingly contradictory statement which nevertheless is true. An analogy (C) is a comparison of two different things that share some common elements. A parody (D) is a kind of satire that ridicules a work's subject and/or style through imitation.

100. C: Realist authors strive to represent reality as closely as possible, even in fiction. They avoid exaggeration, which satire often employs to ridicule social behaviors. Though irony is particularly key in satire, realists often use it as well, such as in O. Henry's "The Gift of the Magi," so choice A is not correct. Both genres may involve writing in a serious tone, ruling out choice B. Jonathan Swift intensifies the satirical effects of "A Modest Proposal" by making absurd and even horrific

Copyright © Mometrix Media. You have been licensed one copy of this document for personal use only. Any other reproduction or redistribution is strictly prohibited. All rights reserved.
This content is provided for test preparation purposes only and does not imply an endorsement by Mometrix of any particular political, scientific, or religious point of view.

recommendations in an ostensibly serious tone. Finally, choice D is not correct because vernacular dialogue is used in both genres, though generally for different purposes.

101. D: This is a simple sentence despite its length. It has only one independent clause, which contains a single subject (He) and a compound predicate with multiple verbs (woke, looked, got, ate, got, drove, parked, walked, opened, went). All other parts are prepositions, prepositional phrases, adjectives, adverbs, and articles modifying verbs and nouns. The other types all include more than one clause—either more than one independent plus at least one dependent clause (A), more than one independent clause (B), or an independent and a dependent clause (C).

102. C: Choice C is correct because a medium's potential for stimulating meaningful audience participation is a major factor in the suitability of that medium for communications intended to promote social change. Though available budget is a factor influencing media choices, it is not the only factor, so choice A is incorrect. Determining a target audience can allow for more informed decision making. This can lead to the development of a more effective message that reaches more people, which is relevant for mass media, so choice B is incorrect. Finally, the duration of a message is influential for media choices, as one medium may be most appropriate for shorter messages rather than long ones, so choice D is incorrect.

103. B: In this paired reading strategy, which improves reading comprehension and helps students identify the main idea in informational text, after silently reading a text selection, the pair of students takes turns following these steps: One student paraphrases what he or she thinks the text's main idea is. The other student agrees or disagrees, explaining why. The pair then develops a consensus as to the text's main idea. Then they take turns finding details in the text that support its main idea.

104. D: She should use the glossaries in the textbooks that were her research sources. Glossaries are alphabetized lists of vocabulary or terminology specifically used in the text with their definitions. These will give the correct spellings, and she can also use the definitions to ensure the correct spelling among very similar words. She should not use the spell checker of her computer's word processing software program because these programs typically do not recognize specialized terminology or vocabulary specific to peculiar disciplines. She should not use a style manual, which she would only consult to find the correct format for citing references and the paper format specified in a particular style (MLA, APA, Turabian, and so on). She should not necessarily use a dictionary before the glossaries in her reference texts because, although many good dictionaries include specialized terminology and vocabulary words, they may not include them all. If she is using specialized terms in her paper that she found in the research texts, the glossaries of said texts will most likely include these.

105. A: Plath opens her semiautobiographical novel by establishing the time, place, and main character's feelings of confusion and disaffection through a statement with literal meaning. This book is not an allegory, and the meaning of its first sentence is not symbolic (B). Its nature is closer to a thinly fictionalized memoir than a historical novel (C). The opening sentence quoted does not use figurative meaning, and the novel is not characterized by any overarching extended metaphor (D).

106. C: The part of speech that identifies a person, place, or thing is a noun (A). The part of speech that describes an action or state of being is a verb (B). The part of speech that describes a noun, tells how many of a noun there are, or specifies one noun as distinct from another noun is an adjective (D). An adverb is the part of speech that modifies (or describes) a verb, adjective, or adverb, making choice C correct.

Copyright © Mometrix Media. You have been licensed one copy of this document for personal use only. Any other reproduction or redistribution is strictly prohibited. All rights reserved.
This content is provided for test preparation purposes only and does not imply an endorsement by Mometrix of any particular political, scientific, or religious point of view.

107. A: In situational irony, things are revealed as other than they seem to both characters and readers, such as when Dickens makes Miss Havisham appear to be Pip's benefactor, only to reveal ultimately that it is really Magwitch. In verbal irony, a character (or narrator) says one thing but means another, such as when Poe has Montresor agree with Fortunato's literal statement that he will not die of a cough; ultimately, readers discover Montresor's true meaning: the cough will not kill Fortunato because Montresor will (b). In dramatic irony, a character knows less than the readers/audience, like Romeo (c). Therefore, (d) is incorrect.

108. D: Madeleine L'Engle (1918–2007) won the Newbery Medal for *A Wrinkle in Time* (1963). Lois Lowry (A) (born 1937) won two Newbery Medals for the historical novel *Number the Stars* (1989) and the young-adult dystopian novel *The Giver* (1993). J.K. Rowling (B) (born 1965), best known for her *Harry Potter* series, has won numerous awards, but not the Newbery Medal (she is British; the others are American). Ursula K. Le Guin (C) (born 1929), best known for her *Earthsea* trilogy, has won a great many awards, including a National Book Award for Young People's Literature, but not the Newbery Medal.

109. B: *Agatha* is the title of a poem written by Mary Ann (or Marian) Evans (1819-1880), who used the pen name George Eliot. She said this was to have her work taken seriously, as female authors during her time were stereotyped as writing only fluffy romances. She may also have used the pseudonym for privacy. Eliot is best known for her novels *Adam Bede, The Mill on the Floss, Silas Marner, Romola, Middlemarch,* and *Daniel Deronda. Emma*, *Pride and Prejudice*, and *Sense and Sensibility* were novels written by Jane Austen (1775-1817), who also wrote *Mansfield Park, Northanger Abbey,* and *Persuasion.* Eliot was strongly influenced by reading Austen's novels. While Austen's treatment was lighter and more ironic and Eliot's more serious and political, both women were famous for their realism, social commentary, character portraiture and analysis, and psychological insights.

110. B: Although passive voice is widely discouraged today, it can sometimes facilitate paragraph cohesion. The passive voice may allow information to presented in a more logical flow. Consider "Specialized teams worked to recover artwork stolen by the Third Reich, but many priceless pieces were lost nevertheless" compared to "Specialized teams worked to recover artwork stolen by the Third Reich, but the world nevertheless lost many priceless pieces from these collections." The passive voice may also provide writers with additional options for arranging words and ideas where active voice would be awkward or distracting. Consider "The Pyramids were built between 2000 and 3000 BC" compared to "Egyptians built the Pyramids between 2000 and 3000 BC." Therefore, passive voice can be useful for paragraph cohesion, and choice B is correct. As demonstrated above, the passive voice does not automatically make paragraphs less cohesive, so choice A is incorrect. Clearly the passive voice is not critical for cohesion, so choice C is also incorrect. Finally, choice D is incorrect because it is too extreme; the passive voice can be used effectively in many situations, not only when it is needed.

Copyright © Mometrix Media. You have been licensed one copy of this document for personal use only. Any other reproduction or redistribution is strictly prohibited. All rights reserved.
This content is provided for test preparation purposes only and does not imply an endorsement by Mometrix of any particular political, scientific, or religious point of view.

Practice Test #2

Multiple Choice

1. A teacher plans to use a rubric to define learning objectives for a class instructional unit, guide students in completing their assignments, and serve as a unit assessment. Which statement is most applicable to incorporating student input into assessment design?

a. So many premade rubrics are available online, it is unnecessary to "reinvent the wheel."
b. Only the teacher, who knows learning objectives and how to do it, should create a rubric.
c. The teacher should collect student input on objectives and assignments to create a rubric.
d. The students and teacher should all work together in designing the rubric collaboratively.

2. A teacher uses a mixture of whole-group and small-group reading instruction. Which of the following activities would be the best choice for a whole-group lesson rather than small-group or individualized instruction?

a. Practice applying specific phonics skills
b. Independent reading of unfamiliar texts
c. Analyzing character development after the teacher reads a novel aloud
d. Spelling patterns

3. According to MLA citation guidelines, which source-specific details should be included for both print and electronic sources: the publisher for books and the periodical title, volume, issue, and page numbers when available for periodical articles?

a. Publisher name
b. Periodical name, volume, issue, page numbers
c. Publisher name for books and periodical title, volume, issue, and page numbers when available for periodical articles, whether the sources are print or electronic
d. Database name, database publisher name, URL

4. A teacher has students read literary nonfiction by Martin Luther King, Jr. To help them make inferences from text, she does a Think-Aloud. Text clues are: seeing a "White Only" sign made King feel sad until he recalled his mother's words, and hearing his father's words when preaching made him feel better. Student knowledge is: parents make us feel better when we are unhappy. Which of the following would be the most appropriate student inference?

a. Seeing segregation signs in his youth made King feel bad.
b. King's feelings and beliefs were influenced by his parents.
c. When unhappy, his parents' words made King feel better.
d. When we are unhappy, our parents can make us feel better.

5. Public speakers want to give speeches that make their audience pay attention, but they also want to give speeches whose messages are meaningful enough to remain in audience member's minds. This can best be accomplished with:

a. Simple language and stories
b. Strict logical progression
c. Sophisticated language and ideas
d. Eye contact

Copyright © Mometrix Media. You have been licensed one copy of this document for personal use only. Any other reproduction or redistribution is strictly prohibited. All rights reserved.
This content is provided for test preparation purposes only and does not imply an endorsement by Mometrix of any particular political, scientific, or religious point of view.

6. What kind of dialect is represented in the character's speech?

"Running after t'lads, as usuald!... If I war yah, maister, I'd just slam t'boards i' their faces all on 'em, gentle and simple! Never a day ut yah're off, but yon cat o'Linton comes sneaking hither; and Miss Nelly, shoo's a fine lass!"

a. Early 20th-century American Southern English
b. English spoken in 18th-century colonial India
c. English spoken in 17th-century rural Scotland
d. 19th-century Yorkshire working-class dialect

7. Which of the following types or purposes of writing generally involves a chronological sequence?

a. Expository
b. Persuasive
c. Descriptive
d. Narrative

8. The phrases "minor crisis" and "loving hate" are examples of which rhetorical device?

a. Hyperbole
b. Anaphora
c. Oxymoron
d. Chiasmus

9. Which of the following structures for essays or paragraphs most often requires an outline to be organized chronologically?

a. Compare-contrast
b. Cause-effect
c. Analogy
d. Process

10. Which of these is most accurate regarding persuasive techniques used in advertising?

a. Repetition and appeals to audience sentiment are both effective persuasive tools.
b. Qualifiers, better known as "weasel words," typically accompany understated claims.
c. Persuasion via humor is used more often in news and advocacy than in advertising.
d. Hyperbole, superlatives, and intensifiers are considered hallmarks of cheap advertising.

11. Among the following, which element is found exclusively in only one genre of literature?

a. Plot
b. Characters
c. Stage directions
d. Rhymed/free verse

Refer to the following for questions 12–13:

Edward Bulwer-Lytton's 1830 novel *Paul Clifford* opens, "It was a dark and stormy night; the rain fell in torrents—except at occasional intervals, when it was checked by a violent gust of wind which swept up the streets...rattling along the housetops,

Copyright © Mometrix Media. You have been licensed one copy of this document for personal use only. Any other reproduction or redistribution is strictly prohibited. All rights reserved.
This content is provided for test preparation purposes only and does not imply an endorsement by Mometrix of any particular political, scientific, or religious point of view.

and fiercely agitating the scanty flame of the lamps that struggled against the darkness."

12. The author's establishment of the setting contributes most to which of the following literary elements?

a. Plot
b. Tone
c. Mood
d. Conflict

13. Which part of speech do the most descriptive words in the passage belong to?

a. Verbs
b. Nouns
c. Adverbs
d. Adjectives

14. Which of the following is a valid guideline for writers of research papers to follow when integrating ideas from another source into their writing?

a. Use quotes to make the most important points.
b. Quote lengthy segments of text to show full context.
c. Focus discussion on the sources rather than original ideas.
d. Use quotes in a way that flows with the writer's own statements.

15. Which of the following phrases is an example of using diction to convey a subjective connotation?

a. a heavy desk
b. a greasy smile
c. a blue sky
d. a formal speech

16. If a writer's purpose is to create portraits of people for a reading audience whose interest is in different personalities, motivations, and their expression in various behaviors and relationships, which mode of writing is most appropriate?

a. A fictional novel
b. A how-to manual
c. A persuasive essay
d. An explanatory paper

17. In writing instruction, what does the process writing approach entail?

a. Hypothetical audiences for written work
b. Students work on their own throughout.
c. Personal responsibility for written work
d. Writing is evaluated only by the teacher.

18. Which of the following statements is correct regarding Standard English?

a. Standard English does not allow for variations of dialect.
b. Rules from standard English apply to written language.
c. Standard English is universal in English-speaking nations.
d. No standard English exists that is actually used in practice.

Copyright © Mometrix Media. You have been licensed one copy of this document for personal use only. Any other reproduction or redistribution is strictly prohibited. All rights reserved.
This content is provided for test preparation purposes only and does not imply an endorsement by Mometrix of any particular political, scientific, or religious point of view.

19. A line manager notices that an employee does minimal work but often seems to be using their smartphone during their shift. The line manager notes that they "struggle with productivity." Which of the following is this phrase, as it is used by the line manager, an example of?

a. Jargon
b. Ambiguity
c. Euphemism
d. Denotation

20. Which of these is NOT a benefit of a well-organized essay?

a. A well-organized essay is more likely to gain readers' acceptance of its thesis as valid.
b. A well-organized essay is more likely to hold readers' attention.
c. A well-organized essay requires less effort to write but more effort to read and understand.
d. A well-organized essay makes it easier for readers to identify the main ideas and the evidence that supports them.

21. When using research-based writing instruction strategies, which should be gradually faded?

a. Brainstorming
b. Explicit instruction
c. Teacher modeling
d. Collaborative work

22. Which of the following methods would give students the most *objective* feedback to enable them to monitor their own performance and progress in speaking and enacting through giving oral reports and presentations?

a. Having classmates offer peer reviews
b. Having a teacher evaluate their work
c. Comparing their work to classmates' work
d. Viewing videos of their performance

23. Of the following components of a reference citation, which one is needed only for citing electronic sources rather than for both printed and electronic sources?

a. Author name
b. Publication date
c. Book/article title
d. The date of access

24. Linguist Noam Chomsky famously composed the following sentence to prove a point: "Colorless green ideas sleep furiously." What element of language use renders this sentence meaningless?

a. Incorrect sentence syntax
b. Contradictory word choice
c. Lack of proper punctuation
d. Subject-verb disagreement

Copyright © Mometrix Media. You have been licensed one copy of this document for personal use only. Any other reproduction or redistribution is strictly prohibited. All rights reserved.
This content is provided for test preparation purposes only and does not imply an endorsement by Mometrix of any particular political, scientific, or religious point of view.

25. What can syntax almost always help a reader deduce about an unfamiliar word in a sentence?

a. The word's meaning
b. The word's part of speech
c. Both the word's meaning and its part of speech
d. Neither the word's meaning nor its part of speech

26. Which strategy can be used to build readers' confidence and increase both comprehension and fluency when introducing an unknown text?

a. Introducing new vocabulary before reading
b. Reading the first few pages aloud before asking students to finish it independently
c. Listing what students want to learn about the topic
d. Asking students to predict what the text will be about based on the title and cover

Refer to the following for question 27:

> Mamzelle Aurélie possessed a good strong figure, ruddy cheeks, hair that was changing from brown to gray, and a determined eye. She wore a man's hat about the farm, and an old blue army overcoat when it was cold, and sometimes top-boots.
>
> Mamzelle Aurélie had never thought of marrying. She had never been in love. At the age of twenty she had received a proposal, which she had promptly declined, and at the age of fifty she had not yet lived to regret it.
>
> She was quite alone in the world, except for her dog Ponto, and the negroes who lived in her cabins and worked her crops, and the fowls, a few cows, a couple of mules, her gun (with which she shot chicken-hawks), and her religion.
>
> Excerpted from "Regret" by Kate Chopin, 1894

27. Which of these quotes from the passage, along with the title of the piece, foreshadows later changes?

a. "She wore a man's hat about the farm, and an old blue army overcoat when it was cold"
b. "she had not yet lived to regret it"
c. "except for her dog Ponto"
d. "her gun (with which she shot chicken-hawks)"

28. In poetry, poems in which form are the shortest?

a. Ode
b. Epic
c. Elegy
d. Epigram

29. When is it most appropriate for students to write in casual language at their own age level?

a. To share a certain experience with their readers
b. To get parental permission for a desired activity
c. To write something for their classmates to read
d. To write a story that younger children can read

Copyright © Mometrix Media. You have been licensed one copy of this document for personal use only. Any other reproduction or redistribution is strictly prohibited. All rights reserved.
This content is provided for test preparation purposes only and does not imply an endorsement by Mometrix of any particular political, scientific, or religious point of view.

30. Which statement is most accurate regarding how writers should integrate evidence from sources into research papers?

a. Writers should summarize each source cited before continuing an argument.
b. Writers should include longer quotations because these have greater authority.
c. Writers should adapt direct quotes to flow seamlessly with the surrounding writing.
d. Writers should add an in-text citation even when paraphrasing rather than quoting.

31. Read the following sentence from an informational text and use it to answer this question.

The Native Americans helped the Pilgrims avoid starvation by introducing them to pemmican, cakes of dried lean meat mixed with fat.

What type of context clue does the author provide to help the reader understand what pemmican is?

a. Definition
b. Example
c. Synonym
d. Inference

32. Which of the following is NOT a characteristic of a strong conclusion?

a. The conclusion highlights that the main points made were meaningful and important.
b. The conclusion includes a restating of the thesis or main argument of the piece.
c. The conclusion brings the work to the expected word count.
d. The conclusion reinforces the main points and reminds the reader how they are related.

33. In analyzing the plot structure of a short story, during which part of the plot does the main character experience a turning point?

a. Exposition
b. Climax
c. Rising action
d. Falling action

34. Identify the grammatical error in the following sentence:

Either give it to him or to me.

a. Dangling participle
b. Split infinitive
c. Adjective/adverb confusion
d. Misplaced modifier

35. In scientific informational texts, which of these are authors LEAST likely to do?

a. Explicitly state their point of view about the research they did
b. Explicitly state the purpose of the research they are reporting
c. Explicitly state their interpretation of the study evidence or data
d. Explicitly state which variables they investigated and in whom

Copyright © Mometrix Media. You have been licensed one copy of this document for personal use only. Any other reproduction or redistribution is strictly prohibited. All rights reserved.
This content is provided for test preparation purposes only and does not imply an endorsement by Mometrix of any particular political, scientific, or religious point of view.

36. The purpose of corrective feedback is:

a. To provide students with methods for explaining to the teacher or classmates what a passage was about
b. To correct an error in reading a student has made, specifically clarifying where and how the error was made so that the student can avoid similar errors in the future
c. To provide a mental framework that will help the student correctly organize new information
d. To remind students that error is essential in order to truly understand and that it is not something to be ashamed of

37. Which of the following sentences is most likely to be a topic sentence of a paragraph?

a. Clearly, the time is ripe for a cultural shift where screens are seen as a necessary evil.
b. Already, increasing screen time has had disastrous effects on public health.
c. Finally, the most disturbing effects of screen time are seen in the realm of neuroscience.
d. Studies also note an unsettling correlation between developmental delay and screen time.

38. William Shakespeare wrote during which historical and literary period?

a. Medieval
b. Renaissance
c. Restoration
d. Enlightenment

39. Which author writes exclusively from one point of view in the book(s) named?

a. George R. R. Martin in the series *A Song of Ice and Fire*
b. J. K. Rowling in her *Harry Potter* series of novels
c. Barbara Kingsolver in *The Poisonwood Bible*
d. None of these uses a single point of view

Refer to the following for question 40:

> "Although we liked Bill and Hillary, we did not go to their party because there were too many people there for us."

40. In the sentence above, which parts are prepositional phrases?

a. "to their party"; "for us"
b. "Although we liked"; "because there were"
c. "we did not go"; "because there were"
d. "because there were"; "too many people"

41. Which of the following attributes of literary characters do authors portray using diction rather than dialect?

a. Ancestry
b. Social class
c. Geographic region
d. Individual characteristics

Copyright © Mometrix Media. You have been licensed one copy of this document for personal use only. Any other reproduction or redistribution is strictly prohibited. All rights reserved.
This content is provided for test preparation purposes only and does not imply an endorsement by Mometrix of any particular political, scientific, or religious point of view.

42. The adaptation of language in a piece of writing to meet the author's purpose or audience is called:

a. Theme
b. Point of view
c. Style
d. Voice

43. Within the genre of poetry, which subgenre is typically a tripartite poem written to mourn a death?

a. Epic
b. Elegy
c. Epigram
d. Epistolary

44. As one approach to gathering student input, what is correct about a K.I.M. chart for learning vocabulary?

a. The K in K.I.M. stands for Know, the I for Identify, and the M for Meaning.
b. Under the K in a K.I.M. chart, the student enters the definitions of the word.
c. Under the K in a K.I.M. chart, the student enters the new vocabulary words.
d. When students make K.I.M. charts, they never include drawings or pictures.

45. According to the ancient Classical definitions, also used by Shakespeare and other playwrights, which of these is NOT necessarily true of the drama subgenres of comedy and tragedy?

a. Comedy is humorous, and it makes audiences laugh.
b. Comedy may not be funny, but it has a happy ending.
c. Tragedy ends in sadness, and it often involves death.
d. Tragedy inspires terror and pity from the audience.

46. Of the following words, which is NOT an example of onomatopoeia?

a. *Hum*
b. *Click*
c. *Buzz*
d. *Moan*

47. Author Frances O'Roark Dowell used a late 1920s Appalachian Mountain regional dialect in her award-winning novel *Dovey Coe* (2000) for the narration. Why might she have done this?

a. The author is most comfortable speaking in this dialect
b. This dialect was natural to the setting and the narrator
c. The unusual language would attract readers' attention
d. It contrasted with the characters, establishing tension

Copyright © Mometrix Media. You have been licensed one copy of this document for personal use only. Any other reproduction or redistribution is strictly prohibited. All rights reserved.
This content is provided for test preparation purposes only and does not imply an endorsement by Mometrix of any particular political, scientific, or religious point of view.

48. In the poem "To His Coy Mistress" (1650~1652), Andrew Marvell writes, "The grave's a fine and private place, / But none, I think, do there embrace." Which rhetorical strategy does he employ in these lines?

a. Satire
b. Hyperbole
c. Verbal irony
d. Understatement

49. A class reads an essay about the benefits to youth of pet ownership. The author's position is very clear: she believes young people should be given the responsibility of taking care of pets. The author cites facts, research studies, and statistics to strengthen her position. This type of writing is called:

a. Expository
b. Narrative
c. Persuasive
d. Didactic

50. Which of these should readers do to evaluate the arguments of informational texts?

a. Identify only assumptions that the author has included in the argument.
b. Word any assumptions identified only from the perspective of a reader.
c. Check if the premises and conclusion in a deductive argument are true.
d. Test for the validity of an argument made based on inductive reasoning.

51. Use the following sentence to answer the question.

I would like to go with you; however, I won't have time.

In this sentence, what part of speech is the word "however"?

a. Adverb
b. Pronoun
c. Preposition
d. Conjunction

Copyright © Mometrix Media. You have been licensed one copy of this document for personal use only. Any other reproduction or redistribution is strictly prohibited. All rights reserved.
This content is provided for test preparation purposes only and does not imply an endorsement by Mometrix of any particular political, scientific, or religious point of view.

Refer to the following for questions 52–54:

O Ship of State

by Henry Wadsworth Longfellow

Thou, too, sail on, O Ship of State!
Sail on, O Union, strong and great!
Humanity with all its fears,
With all the hopes of future years,
Is hanging breathless on thy fate!
We know what Master laid thy keel,
What Workmen wrought thy ribs of steel,
Who made each mast, and sail, and rope,
What anvils rang, what hammers beat,
In what a forge and what a heat
Were shaped the anchors of thy hope!
Fear not each sudden sound and shock,
'Tis of the wave and not the rock;
'Tis but the flapping of the sail,
And not a rent made by the gale!
In spite of rock and tempest's roar,
In spite of false lights on the shore,
Sail on, nor fear to breast the sea!
Our hearts, our hopes, are all with thee.
Our hearts, our hopes, our prayers, our tears,
Our faith triumphant o'er our fears,
Are all with thee,—are all with thee!

52. Overall, this poem is an example of the use of which literary figurative language?

a. A single metaphor
b. Extended metaphor
c. A simile
d. Vivid imagery

53. What is the meter of this poem?

a. Iambic pentameter
b. Anapestic tetrameter
c. Iambic tetrameter
d. Dactylic dimeter

54. How do the rhyme and meter of this poem contribute to its meaning?

a. Their regularity reinforces the idea of steady strength.
b. Their unevenness emphasizes the theme of insecurity.
c. Their monotony establishes a sense of the unchanging.
d. Their choppiness mirrors the images of the stormy sea.

Copyright © Mometrix Media. You have been licensed one copy of this document for personal use only. Any other reproduction or redistribution is strictly prohibited. All rights reserved.
This content is provided for test preparation purposes only and does not imply an endorsement by Mometrix of any particular political, scientific, or religious point of view.

55. Which of the following most accurately defines information literacy?

a. The set of skills required for reading and comprehending information
b. The set of skills necessary to amass a comprehensive base of knowledge
c. The set of skills required for the finding, retrieval, analysis, and use of information
d. The set of skills necessary for effectively communicating information to others

56. A teacher asked his students to prepare a presentation that could be shown in a foreign country. He advised them to

a. use idioms.
b. avoid anecdotes local to the foreign country.
c. avoid quotes from a foreign national of the country.
d. keep the presentation simple and succinct.

57. A number of verb forms are used in headlines. These include simple tenses, infinitive forms, and auxiliary verbs dropped in the passive voice. Which headline below uses a simple tense?

a. LOST DOG RETURNS
b. GOVERNOR TO VISIT CITY
c. GRADUATE NAMED VALEDICTORIAN
d. HERO GIVEN AWARD

58. To help students select the content and format they will use in writing, what should teachers include in their instruction?

a. They should have students consider swaying reader opinions more than giving proof.
b. They should have students consider what readers will agree with instead of disagree with.
c. They should have students consider not what to impart, but what their readers know.
d. They should have students consider what information their readers share in common with them.

59. According to research into vocabulary instruction methods, which of the following aspects is NOT identified as requiring further investigation?

a. Receptive vocabulary vs. productive vocabulary
b. Written and print vocabulary vs. spoken vocabulary
c. Vocabulary definitions vs. vocabulary contexts
d. Depth of vocabulary vs. breadth of vocabulary

60. Which of the following authors was a 19th-century British novelist and short-story writer?

a. O. Henry
b. Charles Dickens
c. Herman Melville
d. Nathaniel Hawthorne

61. Authors Annie Sebold in *The Lovely Bones* and Markus Zusak in *The Book Thief* both use which of these viewpoints or voices to narrate their novels?

a. The third-person omniscient narrator
b. The first-person omniscient narrator
c. The first-person limited narrator
d. The third-person limited narrator

Copyright © Mometrix Media. You have been licensed one copy of this document for personal use only. Any other reproduction or redistribution is strictly prohibited. All rights reserved.
This content is provided for test preparation purposes only and does not imply an endorsement by Mometrix of any particular political, scientific, or religious point of view.

62. A middle school student notices the vocabulary words *retroactive, retrograde, retrospect, retrospective, retrovirus, retro-rockets,* and *"retro" fashions* in reading school and everyday materials. By knowing the meaning of at least one of these words, the student can determine that the prefix *retro-* means which of the following?

a. Backward
b. Forward
c. Sideways
d. Upward

63. A sentence with two independent and two dependent clauses would be most accurately classified as which of the following?

a. Simple
b. Complex
c. Compound
d. Compound–complex

64. Which of the following is NOT one of the purposes of the conclusion in an essay?

a. To summarize the main points in the body of the essay
b. To clarify the context or application of the essay content
c. To reiterate the thesis that was stated in the introduction
d. To include important material that would not fit elsewhere

65. In *Romeo and Juliet,* Shakespeare writes Romeo's line, "What light from yonder window breaks?" What is the syntax of this sentence?

a. Subject-object-verb
b. Subject-verb-object
c. Object-subject-verb
d. Verb-object-subject

66. When reading an expository text, the reader would most appropriately draw which kinds of inferences?

a. Cause-and-effect and/or problem-solution
b. What events occurred and what people did
c. What the author wants readers to believe
d. Ideas that support the author's message

67. Which of the following is the best definition of paragraph cohesion?

a. Each idea is supported with solid evidence.
b. The ideas fit together and flow from one to the next.
c. A topic sentence starts the paragraph, and a closing sentence ends it.
d. All the sentences in the paragraph include appropriate transition words.

68. Which of the following mediums is NOT often written in the second-person?

a. Novels
b. Song lyrics
c. Advertisements
d. Instruction manuals

Copyright © Mometrix Media. You have been licensed one copy of this document for personal use only. Any other reproduction or redistribution is strictly prohibited. All rights reserved.
This content is provided for test preparation purposes only and does not imply an endorsement by Mometrix of any particular political, scientific, or religious point of view.

69. Which of the following statements most accurately compares the components of speeches and the components of essays?

a. Speeches and essays have similar introductions.
b. Speeches provide supporting evidence in greater detail than essays do.
c. The conclusion of a speech must be more forceful and engaging than the conclusion of an essay.
d. Speeches may include greetings, mentions of honored guests, and thanks, but essays should not include these elements.

70. What is a primary distinction between the fiction subgenres of historical fiction and science fiction?

a. One is set in the real past; the other is set in the possible future.
b. One is based on facts; the other is based on speculations.
c. One is concerned with events; the other is concerned with inventions.
d. Answers (A) and (B) both apply; (C) is not necessarily true.

71. Suppose a written or spoken argument's claim is that community colleges in your state have recently had their budgets cut. Which of these would be sufficient evidence to prove this claim?

a. Citing the largest budget cut at one college
b. Citing two prominent examples of the cuts
c. Citing examples from 15 of the 34 community colleges in the state
d. Citing specific cut amounts at all 34 colleges

72. In the word transcontinental, what does the prefix trans most nearly mean?

a. Across
b. Change
c. Carrying
d. Different

73. Which of the following is a difference in form between the Petrarchan sonnet and the Shakespearean sonnet?

a. Both types end with summaries, but only one provides a turn.
b. One type gives a summary at the end, but the other one does not.
c. Each sonnet type has a different total number of stanzas and lines.
d. The two types use different rhyme schemes and numbers of stanzas.

74. Which author was among the founders of the Modernist movement and authored *A Room of One's Own* in 1929?

a. Fyodor Dostoevsky
b. Francis Bacon
c. Charles Dickens
d. Virginia Woolf

Refer to the following for questions 75–76:

African-American youth are more likely to miss school because they face more barriers to attendance, such as logistical challenges (such as unreliable transportation), school suspension/expulsion or residential instability (consider homelessness or frequent moves). Fortunately, there is an old proverb that guides us to the solution: it takes a village to ensure

Copyright © Mometrix Media. You have been licensed one copy of this document for personal use only. Any other reproduction or redistribution is strictly prohibited. All rights reserved.
This content is provided for test preparation purposes only and does not imply an endorsement by Mometrix of any particular political, scientific, or religious point of view.

that all children, especially African-American children, are present in order to learn and develop on a consistent basis.

—Lauren Mims, Fellow, White House Initiative on Educational Excellence, HOMEROOM—official US Department of Education blog, 10/07/2015

75. How does this author provide textual evidence of the barriers to attendance she mentions?

a. She does not provide any evidence of them.
b. She provides it with parenthetical examples.
c. She provides it by alluding to an old proverb.
d. She provides it only by implicit assumptions.

76. Which barriers to attendance for African American students does the author provide examples of here?

a. Logistical challenges
b. Suspension/expulsion
c. Residential instability
d. Both logistical challenges and residential instability but not suspension/expulsion

77. A student who is a non-native speaker of English hands in a composition that includes the following sentences:

Yesterday I go to the park. I have a good time swimming on the pool.

Which kinds of errors did the student make?

a. Subject/verb agreement and word order
b. Verb tense and preposition use
c. Misplaced modifier and sentence fragment
d. Pronoun error and dangling modifier

78. For making speeches, which nonverbal behaviors enhance audience perceptions of speaker credibility?

a. Making eye contact with certain listeners
b. Making random/unrelated body motions
c. Making startling/novel facial expressions
d. Making gestures congruent with meaning

79. Regarding story events in literary fiction, what is many authors' experience?

a. Story events help readers understand event causality instead of motives.
b. Story events are mental experiments that enable exploration for readers.
c. Story events most often define a specific meaning in life or a way of living.
d. Story events can explain motives and causes yet nothing of life's meaning.

80. Among the following, which describes a characteristic that the literary genres of satire and realism both share in common?

a. Ethical issues are often addressed.
b. Behaviors are often exaggerated.
c. Language used is straightforward.
d. Exposure wins over verisimilitude.

Copyright © Mometrix Media. You have been licensed one copy of this document for personal use only. Any other reproduction or redistribution is strictly prohibited. All rights reserved.
This content is provided for test preparation purposes only and does not imply an endorsement by Mometrix of any particular political, scientific, or religious point of view.

81. Which of the following statements adheres to Information Literacy Standards?

a. Students accessing information must critically evaluate it and its sources before using it.
b. Students accessing information should acquire as much information as possible about their topic.
c. Students accessing information efficiently sacrifice incidental learning.
d. Students accessing information must avoid using it for purposes it was not meant to serve.

82. In text coding and text monitoring, which of the following codes means that the student is "really confused" about something in an informational text?

a. ??
b. ?
c. L
d. RR

Refer to the following for question 83:

> A class will visit an assisted living facility to interview residents about their lives. Each group of three has selected a theme such as love, work, or personal accomplishment and written several questions around that theme. Next each group practices interviewing one another. The teacher then asks all the students to discuss the questions that caused them to respond most thoughtfully, as well as those they were less inspired by. The students decided the questions that were easiest to respond to were those that asked for very specific information; for example, one inspiring question was, "Please tell me about something you learned to do as a child that affected the direction of your life." Those that were uninspiring were too broad, for example, "Please tell me about your happiest memory."

83. After they interview the residents, each group of three students will work together to write a piece about the resident. This kind of approach is called:

a. Collaborative learning
b. Companion learning
c. Bonded learning
d. Group learning

84. Which of the following does NOT involve a reader evaluating the methods of appeal used by the author of a text?

a. Paraphrasing, summarizing, or outlining the text
b. Determining a method of appeal that would be better
c. Researching the topic along with unfamiliar vocabulary
d. Considering the types of appeals the author uses and why

85. When an author uses rhetoric to support his or her point of view or purpose in an informational text, by which of these means can they best provide supporting evidence?

a. Relating personal anecdotes
b. Making analogies to clarify ideas
c. Describing relevant case studies
d. Laying out premises and conclusions

Copyright © Mometrix Media. You have been licensed one copy of this document for personal use only. Any other reproduction or redistribution is strictly prohibited. All rights reserved.
This content is provided for test preparation purposes only and does not imply an endorsement by Mometrix of any particular political, scientific, or religious point of view.

86. What have studies found about how teachers interpret and apply research to reading instruction challenges?

a. Teachers make data-based instructional decisions better individually than in small groups.
b. Teachers are generally better at data comprehension than data location in graphs or tables.
c. Teachers do far better at interpreting relationships among variables than question-posing.
d. Teachers plan differentiated instruction better with real (not hypothetical) student scores.

87. Through the structure of his poem, "Proem: To the Brooklyn Bridge" (1930), Hart Crane conveys and reinforces senses of which of the following?

a. Stability, regularity, and connection
b. Impermanence, change, and insecurity
c. Irregularity, chaos, and confusion
d. Eternity free of progress and/or change

88. *Who's Afraid of Virginia Woolf?* was written by which of the following?

a. Mother Goose
b. Virginia Woolf
c. Harold Pinter
d. Edward Albee

89. In an analogy comparing an essay to a table, how would parts of the table correspond to parts of the essay?

a. Each leg is a main idea while the top is all of the supporting evidence.
b. The top is the main idea, and each leg is a group of supporting details.
c. Each leg is one paragraph, and the top of the table is the central idea.
d. The top is the introductory paragraph, and the legs are all the other paragraphs.

90. Among the following reasons that readers must deduce informational author purposes and motivations for writing, which is most important for identifying purposes an author may have had but did not state in the text?

a. Determining an author's purpose enables readers to know what to expect from the text.
b. Discovering the author's motivation for writing allows readers to read for relevant details.
c. Knowing author motivation and purpose enables critical reader evaluation of author and text.
d. When authors define purposes contradicting some text, they may have hidden agendas.

91. Suppose a student writes "My dog is not very bright" as a main point in a composition. Which of the following is an example of additional information that supports this point?

a. "Every time I leave the house to go to school, he cries."
b. "When I come home every day, he is always happy to see me."
c. "At the age of 5 years, he still does not answer to his name."
d. "He loves to play fetch and will not tire of the game for hours."

92. Which of the following should writers of fiction NOT do when writing dialogue?

a. Supply exposition in a subtle way
b. Imitate a real-life conversation verbatim
c. Use nonstandard spellings to show dialect
d. Provide more than a short break from narrative

Copyright © Mometrix Media. You have been licensed one copy of this document for personal use only. Any other reproduction or redistribution is strictly prohibited. All rights reserved.
This content is provided for test preparation purposes only and does not imply an endorsement by Mometrix of any particular political, scientific, or religious point of view.

93. Which of these statements about figurative language in informational text is accurate?

a. Literal language is to denotation as figurative language is to connotation.
b. Due to the purpose of informational text, there is no place for figurative language in it.
c. Both literal and figurative language must be used for effective informational text.
d. Informational text only uses literal language and only word denotations.

94. In "Old Times on the Mississippi" (1876), Mark Twain writes, "I... could have hung my hat on my eyes, they stuck out so far." This is an example of which literary device?

a. Third-person narrative
b. Personification
c. Hyperbole
d. Irony

95. The first paragraph of Abraham Lincoln's Gettysburg Address is a single sentence that reads: "Four score and seven years ago our fathers brought forth, on this continent, a new nation, conceived in Liberty, and dedicated to the proposition that all men are created equal." In the two-column notes active reading strategy, which of the following phrases from this introduction would go in the main idea column?

a. "Four score and seven years ago"
b. "...our fathers brought forth... a new nation"
c. "...conceived in Liberty"
d. "...dedicated to the proposition that all men are created equal."

96. Which of these is an example of poor focus that makes a paragraph ineffective?

a. Unclear transitions
b. Too few main ideas
c. Irrelevant sentences
d. A lack of solid evidence

97. Which of these is a term that is NOT typically used about a literary dramatic work?

a. Act
b. Scene
c. Stanza
d. Chapter

98. Which of the following statements correctly describes research findings regarding effective writing instruction techniques?

a. Teacher modeling and think-alouds are effective.
b. Providing students with scaffolding can slow learning.
c. Exposing students to the processes of writing is sufficient.
d. Implicit and embedded instruction is better than explicit instruction.

Copyright © Mometrix Media. You have been licensed one copy of this document for personal use only. Any other reproduction or redistribution is strictly prohibited. All rights reserved.
This content is provided for test preparation purposes only and does not imply an endorsement by Mometrix of any particular political, scientific, or religious point of view.

99. Use the following sentence to answer this question.

Joseph raised his hand to answer the question, but he hesitated when the teacher called on him.

In this sentence, what is suggested by the connotation of the word "hesitated"?

A. Joseph thought he might be wrong.
b. Joseph did not want to be called on.
c. Joseph was distracted by something.
d. Joseph paused to reflect on the topic.

100. Among the following major types of conflicts typically included in literary plots, which one is classified as an internal conflict?

a. Man against man
b. Man against nature
c. Man against society
d. Man against himself

101. Which of the following statements best explains how students should choose a particular form of writing to fit their purpose?

a. Students who want to get readers to agree with them should use argumentative writing.
b. Students who want to tell a story and the lesson it affords should use speculative writing.
c. Students who want to invite readers to explore ideas should use descriptive writing.
d. Students who want to share an experience with readers should use informative writing.

102. The historical and social context of Arthur Miller's play *The Crucible* is informed by which of the following?

a. The 17th-century Salem witch trials
b. The 1950s communism "Red Scare"
c. *The Crucible* is informed by A and B
d. None of these informs *The Crucible*

103. The following question is based on the first sentence of Ernest Hemingway's short story "The Short Happy Life of Francis Macomber" (1936)

It was now lunch time and they were all sitting under the double green fly of the dining tent pretending that nothing had happened.

The way Hemingway begins this story gives textual evidence of which literary device?

a. First-person narrative
b. *Deus ex machina*
c. *In medias res*
d. *Duodecimo*

104. Which pair contains terms typically applied to two subgenres of *two different* literary genres, rather than to two subgenres of the *same single* literary genre?

a. Picaresque and epistolary
b. Historical and speculative
c. Persuasive and expository
d. Bildungsroman and elegy

Copyright © Mometrix Media. You have been licensed one copy of this document for personal use only. Any other reproduction or redistribution is strictly prohibited. All rights reserved.
This content is provided for test preparation purposes only and does not imply an endorsement by Mometrix of any particular political, scientific, or religious point of view.

105. Which of the following statements applies to presenting information clearly in a written speech?

a. A speechwriter need not define the purpose of a speech beforehand.
b. Logical organization may be sacrificed to prioritize audience engagement.
c. Making an outline of a speech causes a rigid structure and may make a speech boring.
d. Grammar and word choice should reflect natural spoken language.

106. The novel of manners is a form identifiable by which of the following characteristics?

a. Use of language that is tailored to different characters and situations
b. Open or honest exploration of emotion
c. Representation of an established social order
d. Prescription of universal codes for human behavior

107. In "The Story of an Hour" by Kate Chopin (1894), in which of these does the author use the plot structure element of discourse, including sequence and selection, to augment reader surprise at the story's outcome?

a. Narrating some events out of their chronological order
b. Omitting some details, like Brently Mallard's trip home
c. Omitting all description of Louise, letting actions speak
d. Options (A) and (B), but not (C)

108. What is one benefit of using a rubric over other types of assessment techniques?

a. Rubrics break down overall scores by criteria, allowing students to see their strengths and weaknesses.
b. Rubrics allow students to track their progress over time.
c. Rubrics help students see how they did in comparison with their peers.
d. Rubrics help identify the types of reading miscues students are making so teachers can provide targeted instruction.

109. In an essay, which part of the introduction should come first?

a. The thesis statement
b. A hook
c. Background on the essay's purpose
d. A preview of the essay's structure

110. From this passage, which of the following can the reader most accurately infer?

Mamzelle Aurélie had never thought of marrying. She had never been in love. At the age of 20, she had received a proposal, which she had promptly declined, and at the age of 50 she had not yet lived to regret it.
(from "Regret" by Kate Chopin)

a. Mamzelle Aurélie was certainly lonesome.
b. Mamzelle Aurélie was quite independent.
c. Mamzelle Aurélie was changing her mind.
d. Mamzelle Aurélie was sorry to be unwed.

Copyright © Mometrix Media. You have been licensed one copy of this document for personal use only. Any other reproduction or redistribution is strictly prohibited. All rights reserved.
This content is provided for test preparation purposes only and does not imply an endorsement by Mometrix of any particular political, scientific, or religious point of view.

Answer Key and Explanations for Test #2

Multiple Choice

1. D: Although there are many ready-made rubrics available online free of charge, and a teacher's selecting one this way eliminates added work (A), it does nothing to incorporate student input. Although the teacher knows the learning objectives and how to create a rubric, the teacher is not the only one who should do it (B): collaborating with students will not only ensure that they know and understand the learning objectives as well as teach them how to design rubrics, but it will also incorporate their input and feedback about curriculum and assessment into the design. Rather than collecting student input and then creating the rubric alone (C), the teacher should work together with all students to incorporate their input (D).

2. C: One of the challenges of large-group instruction is meeting the needs of diverse learners. Reading a novel aloud helps to make the content accessible to all learners. If students were to read it independently, as in choice B, the text would likely not be challenging enough for some readers and too difficult for others. Therefore, basing a comprehension lesson on a book that was read aloud assists all students with participating. While teachers sometimes introduce and practice phonics skills in large groups, students are likely to have differing skill levels in this area. Proficient first-grade readers, for example, may read consonant blends and digraphs with ease, which struggling readers may still be learning the alphabetic principle. Students in a classroom are also likely to have vastly different spelling skills, making the need for differentiation important.

3. C: In MLA format, books include the publisher's name, and periodical articles include the periodical title and, when available, the volume number, issue number, and page numbers, regardless of whether the source is print or electronic. Choice A is incomplete because it addresses only books, and choice B is incomplete because it addresses only periodical articles. Choice D is incorrect because database information and URLs apply only to certain electronic sources and are not the source-specific details required for all sources.

4. B: This is the only choice representing an inference because the students have to draw this conclusion based on clues in the text combined with their own existing knowledge. The other choices are the material the students have from the text and their own background knowledge.

5. A: Audience members are most likely to retain the points of a speech or lecture if they are offered in the form of a story and the speaker uses language that is simple and direct enough to be transparent. The stories need to be simple, and must drive the speech directly toward an essential and clear point. Including anecdotes is most effective when the speaker uses storytelling techniques that will bring them alive, such as varying pace, pitch, and intensity, using body language to suggest a change in speakers, and using the stage to suggest a setting.

6. D: This quotation is dialogue spoken by the servant Joseph in the 1847 novel *Wuthering Heights* by Emily Brontë. It is typical of the English spoken by the working class in Yorkshire, the largest county in Northern England, during the 19th century. People in the American South during the early 20th century did not speak this way. Examples of their speech can be found in Harper Lee's novel *To Kill a Mockingbird* (1960), which represents Southern American dialect during the 1930s. Colonial Indian English dialects vary widely phonologically, to the extent that they are not mutually understandable, including Babu, Butler/Bearer, Bazaar, and Hindi English. None of these sounds like the dialect in the quotation. Despite the use of the word "lass," the quotation's dialect does not represent rural Scottish dialect.

Copyright © Mometrix Media. You have been licensed one copy of this document for personal use only. Any other reproduction or redistribution is strictly prohibited. All rights reserved.
This content is provided for test preparation purposes only and does not imply an endorsement by Mometrix of any particular political, scientific, or religious point of view.

7. D: Choice D is correct, as narrative writing is writing that tells the reader a story—which by definition involves a sequence of events. Choice A is incorrect, as expository writing aims to give information or explanations but need not and often does not involve a chronological sequence. Persuasive writing tries to convince readers to agree with the author's opinion or position regarding a topic. It also is not generally based on a chronological sequence, so choice B is incorrect. Descriptive writing seeks to paint verbal pictures that convey the natured of places, events, people, or objects to readers. Descriptive writing is more like a snapshot, and does not generally involve a chronological sequence, so choice C is incorrect.

8. C: Choice C is correct because these two phrases are examples of oxymoron, a literary and rhetorical device where contrasting or conflicting ideas are combined to enable deeper exploration of semantics or to create a more striking, memorable, or effective expression of meaning. The other choices are incorrect because they refer to other rhetorical devices. Hyperbole (A) is a blatant exaggeration made for effect, such as "I ate my weight at the buffet today." Anaphora (B) is the repetition of a pattern; famous examples include the opening of *A Tale of Two Cities* ("It was the best of times, it was the worst of times, it was the age of wisdom, it was the age of foolishness"). Chiasmus (D) is the juxtaposition of patterns that are repetitions or inversions of each other, as in John F. Kennedy's famous quote "Ask not what your country can do for you; ask what you can do for your country."

9. D: Choice D is correct because a process essay or paragraph describes or explains some progression, most often in chronological sequence. Choice A is incorrect because a compare-contrast essay or paragraph is organized either by the two things it compares or by the points on which two things are being compared. Choice B is incorrect because, although cause-effect structures may require chronological organization some of the time, they rely more heavily on logic and may involve describing causal factors that are difficult to organize chronologically. Choice C is incorrect, as analogy structures follow similar organization to compare-contrast structures, which are not organized chronologically.

10. A: Repetition—of words, phrases, sounds, images, or ideas—and appeal to sentiment are both effective tools of persuasion. Repetition causes consumers to better recall information, regardless of their response to the message itself. Appeal to sentiment taps into consumers' emotions, making consumers more likely to engage with the content. Choice B is incorrect because "weasel words" that qualify claims tend to be needed for overstated claims rather than understated ones. Choice C is incorrect because advertising uses humor to persuade more often than news or advocacy. Choice D is incorrect because hyperbole, superlatives, and intensifiers are used frequently across the advertising world and do not reflect anything about the quality of the advertising content in which they are used.

11. C: Only the genre of drama includes stage directions, which tell actors where, how, and what they should do physically in plays, which are written to be performed. Plots (A) are found in plays, novels, short stories, and even some poems. Characters (B) are also found in all of these genres. And many plays, particularly early (e.g., ancient Greek; Shakespeare's and other Elizabethan/Renaissance playwrights' work, etc.) as well as some modern and postmodern ones, are written in rhymed and/or free verse (D).

12. C: Though the first clause of this sentence has been widely maligned, ridiculed, parodied, praised, imitated, and even made the basis of literary contests for both bad and good writing, it and the rest of the sentence do establish the setting such that it contributes greatly to mood, i.e., the emotions it evokes in readers. It does not contribute to plot (A) because it includes no actions or events yet. It does not contribute to tone (B), which reflects the attitude of the author rather than

Copyright © Mometrix Media. You have been licensed one copy of this document for personal use only. Any other reproduction or redistribution is strictly prohibited. All rights reserved.
This content is provided for test preparation purposes only and does not imply an endorsement by Mometrix of any particular political, scientific, or religious point of view.

evoking an attitude in the reader. It does not contribute to conflict (D) in the same way it does not contribute to plot.

13. D: The arguably most descriptive words in this sentence are adjectives: dark, stormy, violent, scanty. Bulwer-Lytton also used verbs (A), i.e., fell, was checked, swept, rattling, agitating, struggled; although the last four of these are descriptive, they are arguably not as descriptive as the adjectives. He used some descriptive nouns (B) as well: night, rain, gust, wind, darkness; yet these are still not as evocative as the adjectives. Of adverbs (C), "fiercely" is certainly descriptive, but it is the only one.

14. D: Choice D is correct because quotes that are integrated into the text of a paper should read in a way that flows with the other writing in that sentence or paragraph. The other choices are incorrect because they refer to practices that should be avoided when writing research papers. The important points of a research paper should be the writer's original ideas. Therefore, they should be made in the writer's own words (A). Long quotations tend to include information that is not relevant, in which case it would be better to paraphrase (B). Discussion of sources should not inhibit or replace discussion of the original ideas in the research paper. Sources are only necessary insofar as they prove the writer's point; they themselves cannot be the writer's point (C).

15. B: Choice B uses *greasy* in a nonliteral way; it does not mean that the smile is covered in grease, but that smile has a quality one might call *greasy* with a negative connotation. While *heavy* can be used with different connotations, when describing a desk, it is likely intended to have the denotative meaning, so choice A is not correct. Likewise, *blue* in choice C and *formal* in choice D use denotative meanings to give objective descriptions.

16. A: A fictional novel is a form of narrative writing that tells a story. In addition to plot and setting, characters are key elements of narrative. In developing characters, authors depict their personality characteristics, mannerisms, behaviors, and interactions with other characters for audiences interested in personalities, motivations, and relationships in stories. A how-to manual is informational writing. The author's purpose is informing how to do something by giving sequential steps, diagrams, and/or descriptions of the order and/or manner in which it should be done, for readers seeking specific instructions in how to complete a process or task. The writer of a persuasive essay has the purpose of convincing readers to agree with a point or argument. The audience is interested in the issue being argued. The writer of an explanatory paper would seek to clarify facts, ideas, or processes for an audience seeking to understand these.

17. C: In the process writing approach, elements include having students write for authentic audiences (A), interact with other students throughout the writing process (B), take personal responsibility for their written work (C), and self-evaluate their writing (D).

18. B: The term standard English refers to a form of English used in an English-speaking country that is reflected in dictionaries and grammar books, taught to English language learners, used in published writing, and so on. Because the rules of standard English are adhered to mainly in edited writing, choice B is correct. Standard English actually includes and allows for a range of dialects, which is exemplified by the fact that what is considered a standard English varies between English-speaking countries, so choice A is incorrect. Standard English is not universal; different English-speaking countries have different standard Englishes, so choice C is incorrect. Choice D is incorrect because edited and published writing generally adheres to some form of standard English.

19. C: A euphemism is an instance of an awkward, unpleasant, or offensive word or phrase being replaced with wording that is less blunt or offensive. Since the line manager would seem to be

Copyright © Mometrix Media. You have been licensed one copy of this document for personal use only. Any other reproduction or redistribution is strictly prohibited. All rights reserved.
This content is provided for test preparation purposes only and does not imply an endorsement by Mometrix of any particular political, scientific, or religious point of view.

judgmental if they said the employee was "lazy" or overly critical and perhaps unkind to say the employee "slacks off" or "doesn't do anything," the phrase "struggles with productivity" gets the point across without showing any disrespect to the employee. Therefore, choice C is correct. Jargon (A) is the specialized terminology of a specific field or group. This example might involve some office jargon; however the same phrase could be used appropriately in daily life and with no relation to a particular field. Ambiguity (B) is when a phrase is not clear and could have one meaning or another depending on how it is interpreted. Although "struggles with productivity" is not very specific and leaves a lot of room for interpretation, the basic meaning is clear. Denotation (D) is the meaning of words that appears in the dictionary.

20. C: Good essay organization has many benefits. First, good organization makes the reader more likely to accept the validity of the writer's thesis, making choice A incorrect. Good organization also helps to keep the reader's attention, so choice B is incorrect. Since well-organized essays typically follow a standard format, identifying main ideas is usually easier for readers, which makes choice D incorrect. Choice C is correct because good organization requires more effort from the writer, but it results in easier understanding for the reader.

21. C: Writing instruction strategies proven effective by multiple research studies include brainstorming to plan before writing; explicit instruction of students by teachers in techniques for planning, revising, and editing compositions; explicit instruction in steps to follow for writing argumentation; collaborative work among students to plan, write, edit, and revise their writing in groups; and teacher modeling of writing strategies. Of these, teacher modeling should be introduced initially and then gradually faded as students gain experience and confidence with practice until they independently apply the strategies consistently.

22. D: Having classmates offer peer reviews (A), having the teacher evaluate their work (B), and comparing their work to that of their classmates (C) are all valuable sources of feedback for students about their performance and progress in speaking and enacting through oral reports and presentations as they give different perspectives; however, video recordings of student performance (D) are the only type of completely objective feedback among these choices because they provide an exact record of what the student did. This enables students to self-monitor, make changes/improvements, and appreciate their own progress over time.

23. D: When citing electronic sources, researchers must include the date they accessed the source in their references. When citing both printed and electronic sources, researchers must include the name of the author (A), the date of publication (B), and the title of the book or article (C).

24. B: Chomsky wrote this sentence to prove the point that correct syntax (A), mechanics (C), and grammar (D) are not enough to produce meaning; semantics (B) must also be correct. The sentence structure and word order are correct in his sentence (A); the period at the end is the only punctuation needed (C); and the verb "sleep" agrees with the plural subject "ideas" (D). However, the adjectives "Colorless" and "green" directly contradict each other: a noun cannot be both; and the adverb "furiously" is incompatible to modify the verb "sleep," which may be done peacefully, quietly, etc. or restlessly, fitfully, etc., but not furiously. Moreover, ideas do not sleep, except metaphorically (e.g., "The latent idea slept in his mind until an experience awakened it.") This sentence provides no context to establish/confirm such a metaphor.

25. B: By observing sentence syntax (i.e., structure, word order, word endings, etc.), a reader can nearly always determine an unfamiliar word's part of speech (e.g., a noun, verb, adjective, or adverb). Therefore, choice B is correct. The other choices either state that syntax nearly always

Copyright © Mometrix Media. You have been licensed one copy of this document for personal use only. Any other reproduction or redistribution is strictly prohibited. All rights reserved.
This content is provided for test preparation purposes only and does not imply an endorsement by Mometrix of any particular political, scientific, or religious point of view.

reveal's a word's meaning (choice A). Both meaning and part of speech (choice C), or neither meaning nor part of speech (choice D), and are therefore incorrect.

26. A: Introducing new vocabulary words will help students decode the words faster when they are encountered in the text, thus assisting with fluency. Recognizing the words and knowing their meanings will also build readers' confidence. Additionally, explaining the meanings of the words in advance will help students comprehend the text when they read it independently. Reading the first few pages aloud without discussion will not help students recognize or understand the vocabulary words, nor will it highlight important words beyond the first few pages. Listing what students want to learn about the topic helps to set a purpose for reading, not explain vocabulary. Predicting helps students activate prior knowledge, make connections, and stay actively engaged in the reading process.

27. B: The text in Choice B, along with the title of the story and the opening of the second paragraph, suggests to the reader that Mamzelle Aurélie will likely either get married or regret not getting married. Although choice A might lead the reader to make an inference that the coat and hat belonged to a male friend or relative who was important to her, it does not hint at any events that will occur later in the story. Choice C may cause readers to speculate about the significance of Ponto, but it does not clearly suggest later changes. Similarly, Choice D does not suggest any specific changes that will take place later, though the reader may wonder if the gun has any significance to the plot.

28. D: Epigrams are composed of one to a few lines of poetry designed to be memorable because of their cleverness, word choice, and brevity. An example is Benjamin Franklin's "Early to bed and early to rise/Makes a man healthy, wealthy, and wise." Odes (A), very popular during the Romantic period, are typically complex and can be lengthy. Epics (B) are long poems telling of adventures and heroic accomplishments. In English language poetry, elegies (C) are poems that lament a death or other sad event.

29. C: It is most appropriate for students to write using more casual language on their own age level when writing for classmates. This applies whether they are writing narrative, argumentation, exposition, or speculation. When students want to share a particular experience with their readers (A), they should write using descriptive form, rather than persuasive or explanatory form, for example. Age/reading level will be determined by the audience. When students want permission for a desired activity (B), they should write using persuasive form, with mature, serious diction and more sophisticated vocabulary to appeal to parents. To write a story that younger children can read (D), they should write in narrative form, using simpler vocabulary and sentence structure; shorter sentences; more vivid, entertaining word choices; a lighter tone; and humor when appropriate.

30. D: To integrate evidence into research papers, writers should keep some practices and caveats in mind. They should not summarize every source quoted because that will disrupt the flow of their own arguments (A). Also, writers should keep quotations brief, incorporating them into their own writing (B). Writers should avoid adapting quotes because it may change the original author's intention (C). Instead, writers should paraphrase the source, being careful not to reuse words or phrases in order to avoid plagiarism. Choice D is the correct answer because in-text citations are necessary for paraphrases and direct quotes.

31. A: The author gives a simple definition directly in the text to explain what pemmican is, so choice A is correct. Choice B is incorrect, as an example context clue would provide an example demonstrating the word's meaning, often using *like* or *such as*. Choice C is incorrect because the author does not give a synonym for *pemmican*. Choice D is incorrect because there are no clues

Copyright © Mometrix Media. You have been licensed one copy of this document for personal use only. Any other reproduction or redistribution is strictly prohibited. All rights reserved.
This content is provided for test preparation purposes only and does not imply an endorsement by Mometrix of any particular political, scientific, or religious point of view.

before or after the word that would help the reader get an idea of the word's meaning based on logic.

32. C: Strength and closure are important principles for written conclusions. Choice C is correct because word count does not necessarily mean the piece is complete. Although length is important and can affect the strength of a text as a whole, it does not affect the strength of a text's conclusion. Choice A is incorrect because a conclusion that highlights how the main points are meaningful and important reminds the reader why they should care about the text's topic, which provides good closure. Choice B is incorrect because a conclusion should include a statement that repeats the thesis or main argument that drove the rest of the piece. This, along with reiterating the main points and how they are connected, gives the author one final opportunity to express his or her message and succinctly illustrate that the message has been well supported. Choice D is incorrect because reinforcing the main points and reminding the reader how they are related is one of the crucial aspects of a text's conclusion and will assist readers in identifying and remembering the text's main points and supporting evidence.

33. B: The parts of plot structure are exposition, rising action, climax, falling action, and dénouement or resolution. In the exposition, the setting is established, characters introduced, and plot background presented. During the rising action, the story builds up to the chief conflict or problem. During the climax or crisis (the high point of the story), the main character's challenge reaches a peak, then a turning point occurs that determines the outcome. During the falling action, the story slows down as outcomes of the character's decisions or actions are revealed. During the dénouement or resolution, the author ties up loose ends, and the story is concluded with an unhappy or happy ending.

34. D: Misplaced modifier. "Give it <u>either to</u> him <u>or to</u> me," "<u>Either give</u> it to him <u>or give</u> it to me," OR "Give it <u>to either</u> him or me."

35. A: Authors of scientific informational text, such as research study reports, are likely to state the purpose of their research. They are likely to state their interpretations of the evidence or data their study produced. And in any acceptable research report, they will always identify which variables they studied, the population in whom they studied them, the number of the sample size, the conditions of the experiment, and the research methodology used. However, they are least likely to state explicitly their point of view about their research, unlike authors of other types of informational text who directly state their viewpoint about the topic and/or their reason(s) for writing about it.

36. B: A reading teacher offers corrective feedback to a student in order to explain why a particular error in reading is, in fact, an error. Corrective feedback is specific; it locates where and how the student went astray so that similar errors can be avoided in future reading.

37. C: The sentence in choice C is most likely to be a topic sentence of a paragraph, as it contains a transition word used for introducing a final main point (finally), and it introduces the neurological aspects of screen time in order to set up supporting evidence and discussion related to this topic. Choice A is incorrect because this sentence has the force and suggestion of real-life application that is characteristic of concluding paragraphs. Choice B is incorrect because it states that there are negative effects of screen time. This suggests that at least some of these effects will be listed or explained later which is consistent with an introductory paragraph sentence. Choice D is incorrect because it appears to be a supporting detail, given the transition word "also" that places it in a series and the narrow focus of the sentence on developmental delays.

Copyright © Mometrix Media. You have been licensed one copy of this document for personal use only. Any other reproduction or redistribution is strictly prohibited. All rights reserved.
This content is provided for test preparation purposes only and does not imply an endorsement by Mometrix of any particular political, scientific, or religious point of view.

38. B: Shakespeare (1564-1616) wrote during the Renaissance (B), which is generally considered to encompass the 15th and 16th centuries. The medieval (A) era, also known as the Middle Ages, was earlier, ending in the late 15th century, and included authors like Geoffrey Chaucer, Dante Alighieri, the author of *Sir Gawain and the Green Knight,* and Sir Thomas Malory. The Restoration (C) period in English literature followed the Renaissance, starting in the middle of the 17th century and ending before the 18th century. It included authors like John Dryden, who wrote poetry, satire, and criticism. The Enlightenment (D) occurred in the 18th century and included the authors Jonathan Swift, Alexander Pope, Dr. Samuel Johnson, and James Boswell.

39. D: None of these authors writes exclusively from a single point of view in the books named. In the *A Song of Ice and Fire* series, George R. R. Martin alternates writing from different characters' points of view in different chapters. In the *Harry Potter* novels, J. K. Rowling frequently writes third-person limited narrative from Harry Potter's point of view, but also switches to other characters' points of view at times. In her novel *The Poisonwood Bible,* Barbara Kingsolver narrates in first person, but sometimes changes to third person for narrating major action scenes in which the first-person narrator is missing or not involved.

40. A: "To their party" and "for us" are prepositional phrases because they begin with the prepositions "to" and "for," respectively. The first phrase modifies the predicate (verb) "go"; the second modifies the dependent clause "because there were (too many people there)": "for" is the preposition; the pronoun "us" is the object of the preposition. "Although we liked..." and "because there were..." are both dependent clauses. "We did not go" is an independent clause. "Too many people" is an adverbial phrase modifying the verb "were": "too" is an adverb modifying the adjective "many," which modifies the noun "people."

41. D: Authors portray individual attributes of specific characters by using diction to represent their word choice, grammar, and manner of self-expression. Authors can portray more collective attributes of some characters using various dialects with distinctive pronunciation, grammar, and vocabulary to represent the characters' social class, geographic region of origin, and cultural background.

42. C: Style is defined as the adaptation of language in a piece of writing to meet the author's purpose or audience. For example, an author writing a humorous book will use a different style than an author writing a biography.

43. B: An elegy is a poem of mourning, traditionally divided into three parts: (1) a lament for the departed, (2) praise of the departed, and (3) solace for the loss of the departed. An epic is a long poem written in stylized language, telling tales of heroic exploits and adventures, and combining both dramatic and lyrical conventions. An epigram is a brief poem consisting of one or two lines and using memorable wording to express some wise, perceptive, or witty observation, sentiment, or adage. Epistolary poems are written in the form of letters from one person to another and are read as such.

44. C: The acronym *K.I.M.* in a K.I.M. vocabulary chart stands for Key idea, Information, and Memory clue. Under the "K" for Key idea, the student enters a vocabulary word. Under the "I" for Information, the student enters the definition of the word. Under the "M" for Memory clue, students often make a drawing or attach a picture, sometimes including written or printed captions, to remind them of the word's meaning.

45. A: Although the popular modern definition of comedy equates it with humor and making people laugh, this was NOT the ancient Greeks' Classical definition, to which Shakespeare and others also

Copyright © Mometrix Media. You have been licensed one copy of this document for personal use only. Any other reproduction or redistribution is strictly prohibited. All rights reserved.
This content is provided for test preparation purposes only and does not imply an endorsement by Mometrix of any particular political, scientific, or religious point of view.

adhered, that comedy may or may not be funny, but it always has a happy ending (b). Ancient Greek, Elizabethan and Renaissance, and modern definitions of tragedy all include sad endings, often involving death (c). According to Aristotle, tragedy should evoke audience emotional responses of terror and pity (d) to be effective.

46. D: *Onomatopoeia* refers to words that sound like the sound they represent when spoken aloud. For example, the sound of the word *hum* resembles the sound humming makes. Likewise, *click*, when pronounced, sounds like a click, and *buzz* sounds like buzzing. Although *moan* does refer to a sound, the word is not derived from the sound of moaning. Therefore, choice D is correct.

47. B: Choice B is the only viable reason to use a particular regional dialect for narration in a novel, among these choices. The novel mentioned is narrated by the titular protagonist, who speaks in the dialect and lives in the place and time where this dialect was common. This reminds readers of the setting's significance to the novel and main character. It is unlikely that the author of a book published in 2000 would be most comfortable speaking a 1920s dialect, but even if they were, this would not be justification to have a character use the dialect, so choice A is not correct. While attracting readers' attention (C) and contrasting the narrator with other characters (D) are possible effects of the narrator speaking in this dialect, these are not strong reasons by themselves to choose a specific dialect for a narrator.

48. D: This is an example of understatement. Using the *carpe diem* tradition as a seduction tactic, Marvell argues that life is short, so he and his mistress should "seize the day" and make love while they can. In the lines quoted, he understates the condition of death by saying people do not embrace in the grave—when they do not live at all, let alone embrace there. Satire is ridiculing people and/or groups to expose and criticize their shortcomings. Jonathan Swift wrote biting satires, including *A Tale of a Tub, A Modest Proposal,* and *Gulliver's Travels.* Hyperbole is extreme exaggeration, like saying "I've told you a million times" or "I have a ton of homework." Verbal irony is using words opposite to their literal meaning: in *Directions to Servants* (1745), Swift wrote, "In Winter Time light the Dining-Room Fire but two Minutes before Dinner is served up, that your Master may see, how saving you are of his Coals"—satirizing servants' habits and poor excuses by presenting them as instructions.

49. C: The author is hoping to persuade or convince readers to either request a pet and/or the primary care of their pet by providing them with facts as well as by using rhetorical devices such as dispelling opposing arguments.

50. C: Evaluating arguments used in informational text involves several elements. One element is to test if all the premises and the conclusion of an argument are true. Choice C accurately states this, so it is the correct answer. The other answers refer to actions the reader must take, but they explain these actions incorrectly. Readers should identify not only the assumptions that the author has stated, but also the assumptions the author has implied but omitted, so choice A is incorrect. Choice B is incorrect because readers should word unstated assumptions sympathetically from what they perceive as the author's perspective. Choice D is incorrect because, for arguments using inductive reasoning, readers should test how strongly all of the true premises support the conclusion, not check whether the argument is valid or invalid, which would apply to deductive reasoning.

51. A: "However" is an adverb when it is used to modify a whole clause, as it is in this sentence, making choice A correct. A pronoun is a generalized word (such as he or she) that can substitute for more specific nouns when the listener or reader will know which noun is being referred to. "However" isn't referring to another noun, so choice B is incorrect. A preposition connects nouns, pronouns, noun phrases, and pronoun phrases to other words; in this sentence, *to* and *with* are

Copyright © Mometrix Media. You have been licensed one copy of this document for personal use only. Any other reproduction or redistribution is strictly prohibited. All rights reserved.
This content is provided for test preparation purposes only and does not imply an endorsement by Mometrix of any particular political, scientific, or religious point of view.

prepositions. Since "however" is not connecting phrases to each other, choice C is incorrect. Although "however" can act as a conjunction, this is only the case when it means "in whatever way that," as in the sentence "However you do it, just get it done." This meaning is not the one used in the question, so choice D is incorrect.

52. B: This poem is a classic example of extended metaphor, an implied comparison that extends across the entire work, describing America's Union ("state") as being like a sailing ship braving the treacherous waters of governance. A single metaphor (A) is an isolated incidence of such an implied comparison within a work rather than one encompassing the whole work. A simile (C) is a direct/explicit comparison, e.g., "The state is *like* a ship." The poem does contain auditory, visual, and tactile imagery (D), but extended metaphor is the most prominent literary device of the poem overall.

53. C: This poem is written in iambic (◡ / = one unstressed syllable, then one stressed) tetrameter (four beats per line). Iambic pentameter (A), with five iambic beats per line, is the most common meter in English verse; all of Shakespeare's verses use it. A specific example is Theodore Roethke's villanelle, "The Waking." An example of anapestic (◡◡ / = two unstressed syllables, then one stressed) tetrameter (B) is George Gordon, Lord Byron's "The Destruction of Sennacherib." Dactylic (/◡◡ = one stressed, two unstressed syllables) dimeter (two beats per line) (D) is used by Alfred, Lord Tennyson in "The Charge of the Light Brigade."

54. A: The very regular rhyme and meter in this poem reinforce the idea of the Ship of State as strong and forging steadily onward despite all perils. Therefore, these are not uneven, and the poem does not have a theme of insecurity (B). Though regular, the rhyme and meter are not monotonous, and Longfellow meant to convey a sense that the Ship of State was steadfast, brave, and dependable/worthy of the people's faith and hope, not unchanging (C). The regular rhyme and meter are even, not choppy; although Longfellow describes a stormy sea as part of the extended metaphor, he does not mirror it in sound or rhythm (D).

55. C: According to the Association of College and Research Libraries, information literacy is the set of skills that an individual must have for the finding, retrieval, analysis, and use of information. While it is required for reading and understanding information, it is required for more than this, so choice A is incorrect. It does not necessarily or exclusively involve retaining a lot of information or communicating information effectively, so choices B and D are incorrect. Rather, information literacy involves knowing how to find information, how to evaluate information critically, and how to apply information judiciously to meet specific purposes.

56. D: For the vast majority of people attending a presentation in a foreign country, English will not be their native language, and many of them will struggle to keep up with a presentation in English, so it should not be complex, or very long. It would be wise to include, not avoid, anecdotes from the country, and quotes from nationals. American idioms should be avoided, as idioms by their nature do not translate well.

57. A: This headline uses the simple tense. In this case, it's the simple present tense. B uses the infinitive form, while C and D both drop the auxiliary verb in the passive voice.

58. D: For writing, teachers should instruct their students to think about what kinds of proof and/or evidence they will need to provide for their readers to agree with their points (A). They should instruct students to consider not only what points they will make in writing that their readers might agree with, but moreover what points their readers are likely to disagree with (B), and how to refute or counter those disagreements to persuade skeptical audiences. Teachers

Copyright © Mometrix Media. You have been licensed one copy of this document for personal use only. Any other reproduction or redistribution is strictly prohibited. All rights reserved.
This content is provided for test preparation purposes only and does not imply an endorsement by Mometrix of any particular political, scientific, or religious point of view.

should have students think about what information their readers already know and what information they will share with their readers (C). They should additionally instruct students to consider what information they and their readers share in common (D).

59. C: According to research from the National Institute of Child Health and Human Development (NICHD, 2000), receptive comprehension vs. expressive production (A), written and printed vocabulary vs. spoken vocabulary (B), and vocabulary depth vs. breadth (D) are all aspects of vocabulary instruction and learning needing further investigation. However, researchers already widely agree without calling for additional study that students must learn not only word definitions, but moreover how words function in different contexts (C).

60. B: All four authors wrote novels and short stories in the 19th century. While O. Henry (A) is perhaps better known for his short stories, Herman Melville (C) and Nathaniel Hawthorne (D) are best known for their novels. All three were American authors. Charles Dickens (B), who wrote many famous novels as well as short stories, is the only British author among these four.

61. B: Both authors use the first-person omniscient narrator in these novels. In *The Lovely Bones*, a girl who has died can observe her living family and provides omniscient narration. In *The Book Thief*, the first-person omniscient narrator is Death, who tells the story of the main character, Liesel, interspersed with his own thoughts and feelings. First-person narrators appear as a character in the story and refer to themselves using first-person pronouns. Both novels are written in first-person, but they are not limited to the perspective, thoughts, or experiences of the narrator, making choice B correct and choice C incorrect. Third-person narrators do not exist as a character with their own thoughts, feelings, and motivations. Instead, they are an outside observer relaying what is happening to the reader. Third-person omniscient narrators refer to characters in the third person and know the characters' inner thoughts, feelings, and motivations. Narrators using third-person limited narration, choice D, tell the story from the perspective of one character, but will refer to the character by name or a third-person pronoun. This type of narrator typically only makes the reader aware of one character's thoughts, feelings, and perspectives, while third-person omniscient narrators may refer to the inner thoughts of multiple characters.

62. A: *Retro-* is Latin meaning backward or behind. Retroactive means acting backward, i.e., upon earlier events (e.g., "Monthly fees will be refunded retroactively to your first payment"). Retrograde refers to moving backward, e.g., planets in astronomy; deteriorating/degenerating in biology, or generally in reverse order or receding. Retrospect/retrospective mean looking backward on previous events. A retrovirus (e.g., the AIDS virus) enables reversing genetic transcription to be RNA-to-DNA to produce new RNA retroviruses by incorporating viral DNA into the host's DNA, instead of typical DNA-to-RNA transcription. Retro-rockets decelerate or separate stages of larger rockets to which they are attached by aiming exhaust toward instead of away from flight direction, i.e., backward. "Retro" fashions are inspired by earlier styles. By knowing the meaning of at least one of these words, the student can determine the meaning of the prefix, and thus of the other words.

63. D: A simple (A) sentence has only a single independent clause. A complex (B) sentence has at least one independent and one dependent clause. A compound (C) sentence has at least two independent clauses, but no dependent clauses. A compound–complex (D) sentence has at least two independent clauses, plus at least one dependent clause.

64. D: While a beginning writer may sometimes regard the conclusion of their essay or paper as simply the last paragraph and therefore include any information and or points that they want to present but cannot fit elsewhere, the conclusion is not meant for this purpose, so choice D is the

Copyright © Mometrix Media. You have been licensed one copy of this document for personal use only. Any other reproduction or redistribution is strictly prohibited. All rights reserved.
This content is provided for test preparation purposes only and does not imply an endorsement by Mometrix of any particular political, scientific, or religious point of view.

correct answer. The true purposes of the conclusion are to summarize the main body of the essay (A), to recall or echo the thesis statement (C), and to clarify the context or application of the essay content (B), as by providing a lesson or extended thought. Therefore, choices A, B, and C are incorrect.

65. A: "Light" is the subject of the sentence. "From yonder window" is a prepositional phrase beginning with the preposition "from," then the adjective "yonder," modifying the object "window," an indirect object modifying the verb "breaks." Subject-verb-object is the typical syntax of most English sentences; Shakespeare changes this by placing the verb at the end of the sentence instead of after the subject and before the object as is most common.

66. A: Expository texts are nonfiction works that give information, like how-to instructions or facts about a given subject. Therefore the most appropriate inferences for the reader to draw would be about cause-and-effect relationships, such as in history books, and/or about problems and their solutions. Reader inferences about what events occurred and things people did are more appropriate when reading a nonfictional biography or autobiography. Reader inferences about what the author wants the audience to believe and about ideas that support the author's message are more appropriate when reading persuasive or argumentative text, wherein the author works to convince readers of a position, opinion, or argument.

67. B: Among the possible answers, choice B is the best definition of paragraph cohesion, because cohesion involves supporting details all relating to a main point and fitting together well. Solid evidence is helpful for making a point (A), but this is not an important aspect of paragraph cohesion. Paragraphs should begin with topic sentences, but they do not need to end with closing sentences, and having a topic sentence and a closing sentence does not by itself equate to paragraph cohesion (C). Likewise, appropriate transition words are important for cohesion (D), but they do not automatically make a paragraph cohesive.

68. A: A work written in the second-person refers to the reader or listener as *you*. Second person also includes the usage of an implied subject, which is the understood *you*. This is rarely used in literary works such as novels, so choice A is correct. The second-person viewpoint is more frequently used in song lyrics, advertisements, and instruction manuals.

69. D: A speech differs from an essay in that it is spoken or read aloud to a live audience, where as an essay is published. Because speeches are given at live events, certain components may need to be included that would not be necessary or appropriate in an essay. These components include greetings (to the audience and possibly to honored guests) and thanks (perhaps to the audience for listening or perhaps to those who have helped or influenced the speaker). Therefore, choice D is correct. Choice A is incorrect because speech introductions differ from essay introductions in that they may include some of the elements above. Choice B is incorrect because the body of a speech and the body of an essay should elaborate and provide supporting evidence in a similar fashion. Choice C is incorrect because speech conclusions, while they sometimes need to include information that essay conclusions do not, must be appropriately forceful and engaging, just as essay conclusions should be.

70. D: Historical fiction is set during some previous period of our history, which may be remote, recent, or anything in between; science fiction is set during the possible future (A) or during an imagined alternative present—either one with scientific, social, and other developments not part of current reality. Historical fiction is based on periods, events, and facts from history; science fiction is based on speculations (B) of what may occur through extending current science. However, both

Copyright © Mometrix Media. You have been licensed one copy of this document for personal use only. Any other reproduction or redistribution is strictly prohibited. All rights reserved.
This content is provided for test preparation purposes only and does not imply an endorsement by Mometrix of any particular political, scientific, or religious point of view.

forms can be concerned with events occurring around and/or to the characters and inventions (real and/or imaginary) could also be included in either one (C).

71. C: Citing evidence of only one budget cut (A), even though it is the largest, is not sufficient evidence because it does not represent a significant proportion of all community colleges in the state. Similarly, citing only two examples (B), regardless of their prominence, does not represent a significant proportion of the total. Citing examples from 15 of 34 colleges (C) in the state shows that the general claim is true for a significant proportion of community colleges in the state. Citing specific cut amounts at all 34 colleges (D) is beyond sufficient, to the point of excess: reading/listening audiences would likely be so bored by this amount of evidence, it would distract them from accepting the claim.

72. A: In the word transcontinental, the prefix trans- means "across." A transcontinental railroad or flight goes across a continent. Choice B is incorrect because, although trans- can relate to change or transformation in words such as transform, that is not its meaning in transcontinental. Choice C is incorrect because carry comes from the root in words like transport, not from the prefix trans- itself. Choice D is incorrect because different is not a meaning of the prefix.

73. D: Petrarchan sonnets have two stanzas (an octave, or eight-line stanza, and a sestet, or six-line stanza) and an ABBAABBA, CDECDE/CDCDCD rhyme scheme; Shakespearean sonnets have three quatrains (four-line stanzas) and one couplet and an ABAB, CDCD, EFEF, GG rhyme scheme. Therefore choice D is correct. Choice A is incorrect because both types of sonnets contain a turn (or change). In a Petrarchan sonnet, the *volta* (i.e., turn) between verses eight and nine sets up the sestet; in a Shakespearean sonnet, the final couplet generally contrasts with the rest of the poem, constituting a turn. Choice B is incorrect because both types of sonnets characteristically include a summary. Petrarchan sonnets summarize or answer the first eight lines (the octet) in the last six lines (the sestet). Shakespearean sonnets summarize or answer the first 12 lines in the final couplet. Choice C is incorrect because sonnets by definition have 14 lines, so Petrarchan and Shakespearean sonnets do not have different numbers of lines, though they do have different numbers of stanzas.

74. D: Virginia Woolf had a powerful effect on the modern novel. Other authors that influenced the Modernist movement include T. S. Eliot, Ezra Pound, James Joyce, and Gertrude Stein. The Modernist movement took place in the late 19th and early 20th centuries. The authors questioned traditional forms of literature and in doing so, wrote novels and poems that were full of modern thought.

75. B: The author encloses examples of the general categories she identifies among barriers to attendance in parentheses. Both the general categories and parenthetical examples supply textual evidence. Therefore, choice A is incorrect. When she alludes to the old (African) proverb (C), which is "It takes a village to raise a child," she is not providing textual evidence of attendance barriers; her allusion is used to support her point about the solution. Since she states categories and examples of barriers explicitly, choice D is also incorrect.

76. D: The author gives unreliable transportation as an example of logistical challenges (A) and homelessness and moving frequently as examples of residential instability (C). However, she does not give any examples of suspension or expulsion (B); because being suspended or being expelled is a barrier, examples of these are neither needed nor really possible.

Copyright © Mometrix Media. You have been licensed one copy of this document for personal use only. Any other reproduction or redistribution is strictly prohibited. All rights reserved.
This content is provided for test preparation purposes only and does not imply an endorsement by Mometrix of any particular political, scientific, or religious point of view.

77. B: The student used the present-tense verb forms go instead of went and have instead of had in describing actions that took place in the past. The student also used the idiomatically incorrect preposition on instead of in. The student did not make any other errors.

78. D: Nonverbal behaviors during speeches influence the listeners' perceptions of the speaker's competence, good character, trustworthiness, and therefore credibility. Speakers should make eye contact with everybody in the audience, not just certain listeners (A). Their body movements should not be random or unrelated (B) to what they are saying (e.g., pacing, face rubbing, playing with one's hair, tapping pencils or toes, etc.), but they should reinforce their verbal messages. Facial expressions should not be startling or unexpected (C); they should be consistent with both the verbal content and the speaker's vocal tones. A speaker's gestures should also be congruent with the meaning (D) of what s/he is saying, to fit with and emphasize the points they are communicating.

79. B: Many authors find story events can help readers understand both event causality and character motivation (A), as well as some of life's meaning (D). They describe story events as mental experiments that enable readers to explore (B) different meanings and ways of living. They say story events do NOT necessarily identify one specific or definitive meaning in life or prescribe one way of living for readers (C), but can define some meaning, shape, and direction in otherwise seemingly random events.

80. A: In satire, authors ridicule human failings, including unethical behaviors; in realism, authors often pose ethical dilemmas for their characters to confront and resolve. Behaviors are often exaggerated (B) only in satire, to make fun of and/or attack them; in realism, behaviors are depicted as closely to real-life human behaviors as possible. Straightforward, everyday (vernacular) language used by real, ordinary people is used (C) in realism; in satire, authors may use a variety of language to achieve desired effects of sarcasm, irony, and humor through understatement, overstatement, etc. Exposing human vices and foolishness is more important than accuracy in satire; verisimilitude (representing reality accurately) is more important in realism (D).

81. A: It is a standard of Information Literacy that students must use their own critical thinking skills to evaluate the quality of the information and its sources before they use it, so choice A is correct. Another standard of Information Literacy is that the student should ascertain how much information he or she needs before seeking out the information, as identifying what information is necessary after uncovering excessive information is inefficient (B). Instead of acquiring as much information as possible, students should determine how much information is needed to achieve a reasonable goal. An additional Information Literacy standard is to access necessary information in an efficient and effective way. However, none of these standards include the idea that students will sacrifice any incidental learning by being efficient in their accessing of information, so choice C is incorrect. Another part of Information Literacy Standards is the principle that students should use the information they find in ways that are effective for their specific purposes; this does not require that students avoid using information for purposes that it was not meant to serve, so choice D is incorrect.

82. A: Text coding and monitoring uses eight codes for students to annotate informational text they read. Four of those codes are included in these choices. Choice A is correct because the "??" code means "I am really confused about this part." The other choices refer to valid codes that have other meanings. The "?" code (B) means "I have a question about this part." The "L" code (C) means "I learned something new from this part." And the "RR" code (D) means "I need to reread this part."

Copyright © Mometrix Media. You have been licensed one copy of this document for personal use only. Any other reproduction or redistribution is strictly prohibited. All rights reserved.
This content is provided for test preparation purposes only and does not imply an endorsement by Mometrix of any particular political, scientific, or religious point of view.

83. A: A group of students working together on a project are applying numerous learning strategies at once. Collaborative learning is a hands-on approach that actively involves students in the learning process. Students involved in collaborative learning typically retain the lesson better.

84. C: While researching a topic and related vocabulary can help a reader make a better evaluation, this action does not require the reader to evaluate the methods of appeal used in a text. The other choices refer to actions that require some form of evaluation on the part of the reader. These include paraphrasing, summarizing, or outlining the text using their own words (A); considering the effectiveness of other methods of appeal (B); and considering the types of appeals the author uses and why (D).

85. C: Choice C is correct because reporting findings from case studies is a rhetorical means of providing evidence to support purposes, viewpoints, or claims in informational text. Choice A is incorrect because relating personal anecdotes is a rhetorical means of appealing to reader emotions and making points more relatable or accessible to readers, but not of providing evidence. Choice B is incorrect because making analogies to clarify ideas is a rhetorical means of explaining by helping readers connect ideas in the text to knowledge they already have. Choice D is incorrect because laying out premises and conclusions provides a logical argument based on deductive reasoning, but it does not provide evidence.

86. D: Research finds that most teachers can plan differentiated instruction based on the findings of studies, and that they do this better when using individual scores of real students than with invented scores of hypothetical students. Research has found that teachers make data-based instructional decisions better in small groups than individually, not vice versa. Studies show that most teachers can locate data in graphs or tables, but have more trouble with data comprehension than vice versa. Research also finds that the majority of teachers have difficulty with both interpreting relationships among variables and posing questions.

87. A: Crane's ode to the bridge expresses great stability and regularity in a construction that took longer than most people's lifetimes. He conveys how building the bridge persevered regardless of weather, human activity, day or night—even the suicidal jump from it of a "bedlamite." He does this through the poem's structure, such as maintaining its regular pentameter throughout. Moreover, whenever addressing and/or describing the bridge itself, Crane renders this pentameter even more regular by making it consistently iambic. He even places caesuras (pauses within lines and words) symmetrically (indicated here by spaces between syllables): "And Thee, across the har bor, sil ver-paced /"; "O harp and al tar, of the fur y fused, /"; or "O Sleep less as the riv er un der thee, /". Crane also reinforces stability and endurance with frequent alliteration and assonance. While Crane does portray the bridge as connecting humankind with God ("And of the curveship lend a myth to God") and eternity, he does NOT equate eternity with lack of progress: "All afternoon the cloud-flown derricks turn.../ Thy cables breathe the North Atlantic still."

88. D: Edward Albee (b. 1925), an American playwright, wrote this drama about how the relationship of a middle-aged couple, George and Martha, falls apart. He is also known for plays including *The Zoo Story, The Sandbox, The American Dream,* and *Tiny Alice.* Harold Pinter, a contemporary (1930-2008) of Albee, was also a playwright but was British. He is most known for plays *The Birthday Party, The Homecoming,* and *Betrayal.* Mother Goose is a fictional author of many nursery rhymes and fairy tales. However, not from Perrault's *Tales of My Mother Goose* (1695), but Halliwell-Phillips' *The Nursery Rhymes of England* (c. 1886) was the traditional tale of the Three Little Pigs. The Disney version contained the familiar quotation, "Who's afraid of the big bad wolf?" Albee's play title is a take-off on this phrase, substituting the name of 19th-20th century British author Virginia Woolf. Woolf's writing frequently unveiled and condemned social pretense by

Copyright © Mometrix Media. You have been licensed one copy of this document for personal use only. Any other reproduction or redistribution is strictly prohibited. All rights reserved.
This content is provided for test preparation purposes only and does not imply an endorsement by Mometrix of any particular political, scientific, or religious point of view.

members of the upper class—Woolf's and Albee's backgrounds. In an interview, Albee said, "Who's afraid of Virginia Woolf means who's afraid of the big *bad* wolf...who's afraid of living without false illusions." (The Paris Review, No. 39, Fall 1966)

89. B: Because the tabletop is the largest and most conspicuous part of a table, it corresponds, in this analogy, with the main idea of an essay or other written composition. Because the legs support the table, they represent the evidence and details that support the top or main idea—not vice versa, so choice A is incorrect. Neither the table's legs nor the tabletop represents individual paragraphs, so choices C and D are incorrect.

90. D: One way that a reader can determine that an informational text author may have had a hidden agenda is if the author's stated purposes for writing contradict other parts of the text. When the reader can identify motivations the author has not stated, the reader is better able to evaluate how effective the text is, whether they agree or disagree with it, and why. It is equally true that knowing author purpose enables readers to know what to expect from text, that knowing author motivation helps with reading for relevant details, and that knowing authors' purposes and motivations facilitates critical reader evaluation of author and text. However, a potential hidden agenda is most related to the importance of discovering unstated author purposes for evaluating text.

91. C: The sentences in choices A, B, and D are examples of details that are off topic and do not supporting the main idea; though they may show a general lack of intelligence by the standard used for humans, these sentences describe behavior that is normal for dogs. However, the sentence in choice C is an example of evidence supporting the main point because it states the dog does not respond to his name, implying he has not learned to recognize it in five years.

92. B: When writing dialogue, reproducing real-life conversations word-for-word could make for a boring conversation and one that does not contribute much to the story or characters. Generally, stories are best served by dialogue that is edited to omit anything boring or irrelevant. Choice A is incorrect because dialogue can be used effectively to give exposition in a less direct way. This can cause readers to engage with the story more by, for example, making inferences. Choice C is incorrect because dialect can help readers identify stock characters and can help make characters more realistic. Dialect is generally achieved with changes to standard spelling and grammar. Choice D is incorrect because generally dialogue should serve the story and should not merely punctuate exposition.

93. A: Literal language, which says just what it means, is analogous to denotation, which is the literal meaning of a word (or its dictionary definition). Figurative language, which adds meaning beyond the literal meaning, is analogous to connotation, which involves ideas associated with a word beyond its literal definition. Choice B is incorrect because some types of informational text, such as advertisements, have a purpose that is well-served by figurative language. Choice C is incorrect because there is no requirement to use figurative language in informational text. Choice D is incorrect because informational text can use figurative language and connotations, just as narrative writing does.

94. C: This is an example of hyperbole: extreme exaggeration to create an effect. In this case, Twain's purpose is to achieve the effect of humor. He describes his reaction, "I was helpless. I did not know what in the world to do. I was quaking from head to foot..." and then elaborates on this description by saying his eyes protruded so far he could have hung his hat on them, which is obviously not literally possible. This is an 18th-century verbal precursor of 20th-century cartoon graphics in which a character's eyes "bug out" unnaturally far to indicate an extreme reaction. This

Copyright © Mometrix Media. You have been licensed one copy of this document for personal use only. Any other reproduction or redistribution is strictly prohibited. All rights reserved.
This content is provided for test preparation purposes only and does not imply an endorsement by Mometrix of any particular political, scientific, or religious point of view.

is not an example of third-person narrative; it is first-person narrative. It is not personification, which is attributing human qualities or actions to inanimate objects or animals. It is not irony, which creates humor, sarcasm, satire, or sadness through stating something in terms opposite to its meaning.

95. B: In the two-column notes active reading strategy, main ideas are noted in one of two columns while details are noted in the other column. The phrase "our fathers brought forth… a new nation" (B) would be considered the main idea and go in the main idea column. "Four score and seven years ago" (A), "conceived in Liberty" (C), and "dedicated to the proposition that all men are created equal" (D) are all details related to the central idea of a newly created nation.

96. C: The sentences within one effective paragraph should all be related to one another and to one main idea. Unrelated sentences in a paragraph show poor focus, so choice C is correct. Unclear transitions (A) will certainly make a paragraph less effective, but they are not necessarily an example of poor focus, as the ideas may all relate to one main point but simply not be connected well. A paragraph should have only one main idea, so there would be no way to have too few main ideas (B). A lack of solid evidence (D) will make a paragraph less effective, but it is not an example of poor focus.

97. D: Literary dramatic works, i.e., comedies, tragedies, and other plays, are divided into major sections called acts (A) (even one-act plays have an "act"), and each act is subdivided into scenes (B). Each scene typically is defined by being in a different place and/or time and/or by involving different characters and/or action. Shakespeare and many other playwrights (e.g., ancient Greek, Medieval, Renaissance, Elizabethan, etc.) composed their dramas in poetic verse, so these include stanzas (C), the poetic version of paragraphs. Chapters (D) are divisions not of dramas but of fictional and nonfictional books.

98. A: Research into writing instruction has led to specific findings on the effectiveness of certain techniques. Teacher modeling and think-alouds have been found effective, so choice A is correct. Providing students with temporary support (i.e., scaffolding) that can be gradually removed as their skills grow has not been shown to slow learning, so choice B is incorrect. Merely exposing students to writing processes has been found to be insufficient in teaching writing, so choice C is incorrect. Finally, explicit instruction has been found to be more effective than implicit or embedded instruction, so choice D is incorrect.

99. A: Choice A is the meaning that the word "hesitated" most strongly suggests, as the word generally refers to pausing, but it often implies that the pause is due to a moment of doubt or uncertainty. Choice B is plausible, because Joseph could conceivably have raised his hand hoping not to be called on. For example, he might've been trying to show that he was participating in class and was not expecting to be called on. However, this is far from obvious, and with no further context, this choice is not the best one. Choice C is also possible, but there is no mention of any circumstance that could cause a distraction, so there is no specific reason to make this inference. Choice D might appear congruous with Joseph's need for more time to think, but "paused to reflect" suggests an action that is more pensive or whimsical than fits with "hesitated."

100. D: Among these major types of conflicts found in literary plots, only one is an internal conflict, while the other three are external conflicts. Choice D, man against himself, is classified as an internal conflict because it goes on inside a character's mind. Man against man (A), man against nature (B), and man against society (C) are all classified as external conflicts because they involve a struggle between a character and someone or something outside that character.

Copyright © Mometrix Media. You have been licensed one copy of this document for personal use only. Any other reproduction or redistribution is strictly prohibited. All rights reserved.
This content is provided for test preparation purposes only and does not imply an endorsement by Mometrix of any particular political, scientific, or religious point of view.

101. A: Choice A is correct because students who want to get readers to agree with them should use argumentation or persuasion. Students who want to relate a story and the lesson to learn from it should use narrative writing, not speculative writing, so choice B is incorrect. Students who want to invite readers to explore ideas should use speculative writing, not descriptive writing, so choice C is incorrect. Students wanting to share an experience with readers should use descriptive or narrative writing depending on the experience, not informative writing, so choice D is incorrect.

102. C: Both American historical and social contexts of the Salem witch trials in the late 1600s and the fear of communists in the 1950s informed Miller's writing of *The Crucible* (1953). Miller used an overt depiction of the Salem witch trials as an allegory for the panic over Communism he witnessed—and was himself victimized by—during the time he wrote the play. This "Red Scare" was epitomized by McCarthyism, when Senator Joseph McCarthy spearheaded prejudicial investigation and blacklisting of many Americans, including many creative artists, for suspected or accused Communist affiliation or activities. Salem and McCarthyism shared parallel properties of government coercing private citizens to investigate and punish an unproven and ultimately nonexistent "threat."

103. C: Hemingway begins the story in the middle of the action. This literary device is called *in medias res,* Latin for "in the middle of things." Its tradition dates to ancient Roman poet Horace's advice to aspiring epic poets not to start with the beginning, but begin with the heart of their story. Textual evidence includes Hemingway's use of "It was now lunch time," implying things had happened before; and "...pretending that nothing had happened," implying something had happened previously. This story does not use first-person narrative which would narrate with "I/me/my/we/us," but third-person narrative ("they," "he," and so on) The quotation does not contain *deus ex machina*, Latin for "God from a machine," a magical or unbelievable mechanism introduced to resolve a plot conflict. (Its origin is ancient Greek dramas wherein gods intervened onstage, often via elaborate machinery.) *Duodecimo* is a bibliographic book format or size, similar to contemporary paperback size (*octavo* is similar to contemporary hardcover book size).

104. D: A bildungsroman is a term for a novel in which the main character comes of age, develops, learns, and/or grows; an elegy is a term for a poem which mourns the dead. Picaresque refers to a novel about the misadventures of a roguish protagonist; epistolary refers to a novel written in the form of letters/telegrams/other correspondence (A). Fictional novels can be historical, i.e., based on actual events and characters in history, or speculative, i.e., exploring not actual/current/historical but potential/future events/developments (B). Nonfictional essays can be persuasive, i.e., aiming to convince readers of a position, or expository, i.e., aiming to impart information (C).

105. D: A few principles are important to keep in mind when trying to achieve clarity in a written speech. Grammar and word choice should be accurate, but the speechwriter should keep in mind that each sentence will be spoken to an audience rather than read by one, so choice D is correct. Choice A is incorrect because the speechwriter must define the purpose of the speech before writing or delivering it. Choice B is incorrect because prioritizing audience engagement will by necessity involve logical organization, as audiences will not be able to follow a poorly organized speech. Choice C is incorrect because making an outline first gives the speechwriter a structure on which to build an engaging speech. Rather than hurting attention, a clear outline increases the chances that audiences will be able to follow all of the points made.

106. C: Characteristics of the novel of manners include the following: impersonal language, inhibited emotional expression, descriptions of the codes of behavior for whichever society it involves, and representation of an established social order (C). The first of these three features are

Copyright © Mometrix Media. You have been licensed one copy of this document for personal use only. Any other reproduction or redistribution is strictly prohibited. All rights reserved.
This content is provided for test preparation purposes only and does not imply an endorsement by Mometrix of any particular political, scientific, or religious point of view.

the opposite of the features described in choices A, B, and D. Some of the best examples of novels of manners are those by Jane Austen (e.g., *Sense and Sensibility, Pride and Prejudice, Mansfield Park, Emma, Northanger Abbey, Persuasion,* etc.).

107. D: Kate Chopin narrates some of the events in this story in a different order than they actually occur chronologically, and this makes the end more surprising to readers. She also omits some details. For example, there is no mention of Brently's trip home until he arrives, so readers are just as surprised as Louise is to see him (B). Chopin does NOT omit all description of Louise; she not only lets her actions speak (C) for her in many instances, but also uses description of her appearance and behavior to inform her character.

108. A: Rubrics are a type of evaluation tool that assign both overall scores and scores in individual component areas of an assignment. In each component area, the criteria used to assign scores for different levels of mastery are outlined. Therefore, students can see their overall grades on assignments, as well as how they performed in each component area. This helps students assess their strengths and weaknesses. Rubrics do not specifically track progress over time, though teachers could evaluate students using the same rubric at different points of the year and compare the results. Rubrics assess individual performance and do not compare students to their peers. Choice D describes a miscue analysis, which is a different type of assessment.

109. B: The first part of the introduction to an essay or paper should be a sentence or series of sentences that will get the reader's attention so that they are interested in continuing to read. Such a sentence or series of sentences may be called an "attention-getter" or "hook," so choice B is correct. Following the hook should be some pertinent background information followed by the thesis statement, which is a clear expression of the main point the writer is trying to make in the essay or paper. Since the thesis statement does not come first, choice A is incorrect. An optional part of the introduction is an explanation of how the thesis will be supported or defended that highlights the main points to follow in the body paragraphs. As this is usually at the end of the introduction, choice D is incorrect. Another optional part of the introduction is a portion that informs the reader of the writer's reason for choosing the essay or paper's specific topic. The most appropriate place for this explanation would be between the hook and the thesis, so choice C is incorrect.

110. B: The reader can infer that Mamzelle Aurélie was independent from the description of her never having thought of marrying, never having been in love, having declined a proposal, and so far never having lived to regret this. Readers cannot infer from this passage alone that she was lonesome (A), was changing her mind (C), or was sorry she was unmarried (D). Readers may infer from the title she ultimately regrets something in this story, but not from this passage alone.

Copyright © Mometrix Media. You have been licensed one copy of this document for personal use only. Any other reproduction or redistribution is strictly prohibited. All rights reserved.
This content is provided for test preparation purposes only and does not imply an endorsement by Mometrix of any particular political, scientific, or religious point of view.